Ferries and Ferrymen in Alberta

by
Elizabeth Haestie

Glenbow Museum
1986

ISBN 0-919224-51-2

For all Alberta ferrymen

Contents

Acknowledgments

A faded photograph of a ferry, tucked away in the back of an old clock, started my research into the history of Alberta's river crossing ferries. Mrs. Levette, who donated the clock to the Glenbow Museum, is gone now, predeceased by many years by her husband, William Levette, onetime postmaster and ferryman at the little post office settlement of Riverbow, Alberta. The ferry looked somewhat crude and home-made, but something about it and the team of horses standing patiently on its deck, awakened my interest in ferries.

Inquiries to various archives, libraries and bookstores for more information met with scant results. However, enough preliminary information was gathered about ferries to make one wonder why nobody had ever compiled a history of them.

This is the photograph which started it all. When the author saw this view of the Riverbow ferry, she was launched into an exhausting study of ferries in Alberta.

This work should have been started many years ago. So many pioneers who would have remembered the earlier ferries are gone and, with the early official records not now available, it was necessary to appeal to the people of Alberta for information, photographs, etc. The response was very gratifying, resulting not only in ferry information from many people all over the province, but many valued personal friendships in the process.

It is, of course, the ferrymen themselves who operated the ferries in fair weather and foul, sometimes with great difficulty and in hazardous conditions, who really merit recognition of their services. I hope that this presentation of Alberta's ferry history will serve as a somewhat belated tribute to all those ferrymen who helped the pioneers and early settlers to reach their chosen land; who made it possible for farmers to get their grain to market; who ensured that mail and supplies reached otherwise isolated communities, that doctors reached their patients, and children were carried to school.

Appended is a list of all the people and organizations who have given their help so generously, and my grateful thanks go to every one of them, especially to the pioneers and their families who have shared their reminiscences, ferry-tales and photographs with me.

I am grateful to the editors of the Alberta newspapers who published my first request for information, and to Alberta Transportation for allowing me to search through some of their files. The staff of Glenbow Museum Library and Archives have given me a great deal of help, and I am particularly indebted to Dr. Hugh Dempsey for all his advice and assistance.

Special thanks are due to the Explorations Programme of The Canada Council for their research grant; to the Alberta Historical Resources Foundation which provided funds for typing; and to the Hon. Marvin Moore, Minister of Transportation, government of Alberta, for a generous grant in aid of publication. Last, but not least, I wish to thank my former employers, the Glenbow Museum, for all their support and encouragement in what has been a labour of love.

ELIZABETH HAESTIE

I
Ferries in Territorial Times

The ubiquitous river crossing ferry has served man almost since the beginning of time. A wooden paddle found in England, dating back to 7500 B.C., indicates the use of some kind of river craft almost ten thousand years ago. The early Egyptians, about 1500 B.C., used boats of reeds covered with pitch to traverse their rivers and canals. The Assyrians in the sixth century B.C. used inflated animal skins to carry themselves and their belongings across rivers and streams; and a relief carving of a Roman vessel about 527 A.D. shows a craft using primitive paddle wheels propelled by oxen on the treadmill principle. Legend tells of King Arthur and his Knights of the Round Table using ferries to cross rivers, and Saint Christopher, the patron saint of all travellers and wayfarers, ranks as a kind of ferryman when carrying the Christ child across the river on his back.

Ferries and ferrymen also appear in myth and legend as transporters of the dead to their final resting places. Ancient Egyptians believed that their souls would be ferried across their last river to meet their god, Osiris, and, according to Greek myth, Charon, the ferryman, carried his passengers across the River Styx to Hades.

Regardless of myth and legend, the actual roles of ferries and ferrymen throughout the ages have been an important and necessary part of daily human life. Ferries in all parts of the world have been used by all manner of people — by kings and queens, church prelates, tradesmen and trvellers, honest men, thieves and murderers — for fair means and for foul. They have carried many and varied cargoes — the living and the dead, mail and supplies, household goods and equipment of all kinds — across countless rivers all over the world as they played their part in the progress of mankind.

A ferry, according to Webster, is "a transportation system for carrying people, goods, etc., across a narrow body of water — a boat for this purpose." The "boat" can be anything from a crude raft of logs to the most modern hovercraft, and ferries of many different designs and shapes have been used in Canada since the first white men arrived. There is little recorded use of either ferries or bridges by the Indians. Apart from their canoes in some areas, their construction of

For countless generations, Plains Indians crossed rivers by making a temporary craft of hides and willows. Known as bull boats, these ferries were cumbersome but efficient.

bull boats — a variation of the ancient coracle — and their use of dirt bridges over the river ice in winter, the Indians used their long established trails and easy fording places. These trails were mostly followed and used by explorers, traders, and early settlers.

Although employees of the Hudson's Bay Company worked and lived in the prairie provinces from the eighteenth century, their records contain only a few passing references to crafts used for river crossings. These were usually small rowboats used for carrying their native customers and others across rivers to trade at the forts.

Early travellers used several methods to carry themselves and their belongings across rivers. A variation of the Indian bull boat consisted of a piece of buffalo hide or a tarpaulin stretched between two circled willow saplings. It carried one, or even two, passengers who sat in the centre of the saucer-shaped craft and either poled themselves across a river or attached the bull boat by ropes or thongs to a horse, which swam across.

Crossings in these makeshift crafts were hazardous as they could not carry a great deal of weight, and the passenger, unless he sat in the exact centre, was likely to be tipped out. If a buffalo hide was used to construct the boat, there was a certain amount of water seepage so even if the craft arrived safely at the other side, the passenger and his goods usually became more than a little damp.

Another method of river crossing was to remove the wheels from a Red River cart and use the body as a floating craft, the wheels being reassembled on the cart once the crossing was made.

A description of using carts and a skin craft to cross the river at Brosseau, on the North Saskatchewan River, was recorded by Charles N. Bell when travelling with a group of Metis in 1872. He stated:

> Standing on the high upper bank of the Saskatchewan, I wondered how we were to cross over to the south shore, for there was neither ferry nor boat to use for the passage, but I was soon to see how the "link between the white man and Indian" could adapt himself to circumstances and overcome difficulties, such as now presented themselves.
>
> No time was lost. The horses drawing the carts were carefully led down a narrow zigzag road to the river's edge where the water, receding after the August, or mountain flood, had left a broad strip of sand-covered boulders. The horses were quickly unhitched, unharnessed, and tethered to the willow brush which in places covered the ledges of the bank. Johnny, Cleophas and I unloaded the carts. Removing the great wooden wheels from the axles and drawing the remainder of the vehicles into the quiet water of a little cove formed by a sand bar jutting out into the stream, we soon had the wheels placed flat on the upper side of the huge, straight shafts, where they were lashed with thongs of raw buffalo hide. The carts, being constructed entirely of wood, floated high in the water, and were all ready for the passage.
>
> McGillies, in the meantime, had placed to soak in the water a great oblong-shaped piece of rawhide formed by the sewing together, securely and closely, of two buffalo hides, which at other times served as cart covers. Placing some large stones on the hides to keep them under water and prevent the rapid current from bearing them away, he joined Francois to lend him some assistance in his work. Francois had cut down and carefully trimmed a number of willow rods and wands, and in a wonderfully short space of time formed the skeleton frame of a canoe, about twelve feet in length, tying and binding the parts together with pieces of shagganappi (strips of raw buffalo hide) which, quickly drying in the warm sun, contracted and became hard and unyielding as bands of iron.
>
> The hides, now wet and pliable, were drawn from the water and stretched out on the level sand bar, when it took but a few minutes to place the framework upon them, fold up the sides about the top rails, pierce holes with a knife along the edges, and firmly tie and lash all together with babische (finely cut strings of raw deer skin used in the manufacture of snowshoes, etc.).
>
> Before I could well realize it, there lay before us, as the result of this work, a good roomy, serviceable canoe, somewhat clumsy it is true, but fairly water-tight, and quite capable of containing a lot of provisions and camp equipage at each trip it made, under the propelling power of a couple of rough paddles, wielded by the strong arms of its occupants. The craft was committed to the water, and without delay McGillies and Cleophas, taking with them a load of baggage, pushed off, and avoiding rocks and shoals, safely landed on the opposite shore, fully three hundred yards distant. Cleophas returned with the empty boat, and we all joined in the task of starting the animals and carts of the voyage across.

During the mid-1800s, the missionaries came to the west where they laboured among the Indians, fur traders and hunters, and travelled widely over rough trails and across the many unbridged rivers, often on foot, sometimes on horseback. The Rev. George McDougall, in a letter to his superior in Ottawa, dated 16 August, 1863, wrote:

> In old times, crossing the rivers with a large camp was a tedious affair. A leather tent or large piece of oilcloth was spread out on the ground and the travelling kit placed in the centre. The cloth was then gathered up and tied at the top giving the appearance of a huge pudding bag. This was then shoved into the water and attached by a line to a horse's tail. The traveller then mounted the horse and guided it to the opposite shore. In this way, many times, I have crossed rivers. We now have a good scow and the novel scenes of yore have passed away.

McDougall did not indicate where his scow was located but it was probably at the Victoria (Pakan) settlement where he was residing in 1863.

Many novel ways of river crossing were used; at one time, McDougall made a crossing with the Rev. Thomas Woolsey in what appears by his description to be a bull boat. His son, the Rev. John McDougall, tells the story:

> . . . a large hoop about six feet in diameter was made out of two willows. A large piece of oilcloth was spread out on the ground, the hoop placed on top of it and the corners and sides turned in on to the hoop. Into the centre of this ring was put all the travelling equipment — saddles axes, guns, ammunition, kettle, frying pan, etc. — and this was floated across the river tied to one of the horses with a piece of

A Metis brigade used the boxes of Red River carts to ferry their goods and people across streams. This 1874 engraving shows several methods of crossing being used.

11

buffalo line. Father and Mr. Woolsey crossed in this manner, sitting in the big "nest" quite believingly . . . the rest of the party each grasped a horse's tail and were towed over.

Again, in a letter dated July, 1874, to the Missionary Committee in Ottawa, George McDougall wrote:

> I visited Victoria [Pakan] in April, then went to Athabasca . . . then to Bow River [Calgary]. . . and last week to Lake St. Ann's. In making these journeys I have forded, rafted, or swam 30 rivers.

John McDougall, on his way from Edmonton to meet the newly arrived North-West Mounted Police in 1874, reported that the Battle and the Blindman rivers "were as great streams and we had to spend a lot of time at each one . . ." When they came to the Red Deer River it was in full spate, and waiting to cross also were John Glenn (the first rancher in the Calgary area) and his party. John McDougall immediately started to construct a "ferry":

> I had with me two buffalo cow hides sewn together with sinew. These I at once put into the water to soak. Then I took the wheels off the only real wooden cart we had with us. With these lashed one behind the other, with the dish side up, I bound them solid with small dry poles. Then I put a side board from the cart from hub to hub, thus making a keel of it. Then I spread the cow hides, hair side up, on the shore and placed our wheel frame fairly in the centre and drew the hides up tight all around. When all was fastened we turned our craft up to dry for a little while in the sun and wind, and when it was dry we caulked the seams and stitches in the hides with the hard tallow of the buffalo, prepared by chewing it in our mouths.
>
> Then we put this drum of a boat — or, as my man said, who had never beheld such a ferry — a "rum craft" — into the stream and began loading and crossing . . . . we put six to seven hundred pounds of equipment and freight on the frail craft and while my men towed it slightly further upstream I stripped to my light under-clothes, caught a horse and fastened a long line to the scow. Then I rode the horse out into the stream and after us came the frail, saucer-like boat.

John McDougall, John Glenn, and the other men toiled and worked like this until they had made nine "ferry" crossings, reloading all the goods and equipment on the other side of the river before they could continue on their journey. As John McDougall wrote, river crossings and struggling with heavy currents "was a great strain on the strength."

By the late 1800s, independent traders and buffalo hunters were establishing new trails, most of which, of necessity, crossed the rivers at comparatively easy fording places. Many crossings are indicated on early maps of the area. On the Battle River, Donald Todd, a veteran trader and hunter, is remembered at "Todd's Crossing," although there is no record of a ferry operation there. Todd's Crossing was just south of present-day Gwynne. Near Duhamel, "Salvais' Crossing" is marked on old maps, where Abraham Salvais (Salois, Solway) operated his own ferry where the Laboucane settlement later flourished. Salvais, a buffalo hunter and trader, was related by marriage to Gabriel Dumont, Louis Riel's friend and lieutenant, who operated "Gabriel's Ferry — The Best on the River" near Battleford in the 1880s.

In 1873, the Dominion Government authorized the establishment of the North-West Mounted Police and, after their long march west, the force caused Fort Macleod to be rather hastily built in the fall of 1874. In the following year Fort Calgary, Fort Saskatchewan, and Fort Walsh were built. By the end of 1875, the police had routed the whiskey traders and transformed almost all of the North-West Territories into a more or less peaceful haven, ready to welcome the inflow of settlers.

Major-General E. Selby-Smith, who made a tour through the North-West Territories in 1875, commented on the need for ferries:

> It is necessary to maintain one rowboat and one scow as ferries upon the Battle, the Bow, and the Red Deer Rivers, as well as the Whitemud and the Blindman, which are often so swollen as to intercept travel for days and weeks together . . . as the country fills with population, bridges will no doubt be constructed.

In 1877 the NWMP report from Fort Calgary stated "the Bow River is broad and rapid and crossings are made by temporary rafts" and in 1877, police account books show a sum of $50 "paid to H. Paquette for a ferry boat for the Bow River."

In 1883 Supt. A. H. Griesbach at Fort Saskatchewan reported that:

> There are six ferries in the district, four of which are run on the tariff supplied by the North-West Ordinances. The two at Edmonton under municipal licenses have a much cheaper tariff of charges. The four others are at Clover Bar, Fort Saskatchewan, and Red Deer. The one at Red Deer was, I understand, not used much owing to . . . the water in the river.

The 1883 annual report of the North-West Mounted Police called desperately for bridges over many small rivers and streams. The opinion of the ferries apparently was not very high, as evidenced by the report:

> The ferries in the north are well and cheaply run in accordance with the Territorial Act, but in the Macleod district there are no licensed ferries, the people positively declining to run ferries for the rate allowed for tolls. The rates charged are frequently exorbitant and the traveller is at the mercy of the owner of the ferry who can, and does, cross him when he is ready and at his own price.

Frequently when the ferry is most required the violence of the streams prohibits their use and small boats of the most primitive sorts are the only means available and traffic is actually stopped for several weeks.

From about 1889 the ferries were reported on annually by the North-West Mounted Police. More settlers were coming into the area and trails were being improved into rough roads. Apart from the substantial bridges in the larger settlements of Edmonton, Calgary, Medicine Hat, and Red Deer, many small wooden bridges had been erected across the smaller streams and rivers.

Commissioner L. W. Herchmer's 1889 report stated that:

Owing to the extreme dry weather, roads all over the Territory are excellent . . . there was very little use for bridges or ferries because the rivers were so low that they could easily and safely be forded.

The 1890 annual report said that:

During a considerable portion of the year the ferries are workable and the crossing has to be made in small boats and over floating ice on foot. Even when working, not only is the inconvenience of ferries great but the public are mulcted out of a large sum of money which a new country can ill afford.

and:

Ferries have been running at Morley, Mitford, and Blackfoot Crossing, all on the Bow River, and on the High River at the Crossing. When not carried away by floods they have been working and are a convenience to travellers, though costly.

Supt. S. B. Steele at Ford Macleod also reported in 1890 that:

. . . there are two ferries in this district, one at Kipp and one at Fort Macleod, both crossing the Old Man's River. The ferry at Kipp has been improved this year but the other is seldom in working order when most needed . . .

One of Alberta's early ferries crossed the Oldman River near Fort Macleod. It is shown in this sketch of 1884.

In 1891, Supt. J. H. McIlree at Calgary stated:

Ferries are the same as last year at Morley, Mitford, Blackfoot Crossing and High River. A ferry was put on late in the fall on the Bow, just below the junction of the Elbow, to enable people to get on to the three islands. It is intended, I believe, to make these islands into a public park.

Supt. A. H. Griesbach reported from Fort Saskatchewan in 1893:

There are 6 ferries in this district, 4 of which are run on the tariff supplied by the N.W. Ordinances. Two at Edmonton under municipal licenses have a much cheaper tariff of charges. The four other ferries are at Clover Bar, Fort Saskatchewan, Victoria, and Red Deer. The one at Red Deer was not used much owing to the water in the river.

Supt. W. D. Jarvis reported from Fort Calgary in 1893 that:

The roads in this district, though very stony in places, are kept in fairly good order. Good bridges have been built on most of the main trails and ferries are also maintained so that travel may be carried on without inconveniences or danger.

A year later, Inspector Z. T. Wood of the Calgary detachment reported rather optimistically:

. . . the roads, bridges and ferries are kept in good order. The ferries are fast becoming a thing of the past, bridges having been built where all main trails cross rivers.

In spite of the fact that Inspector Wood already saw ferries as fast becoming outmoded, they continued to operate where required; in fact, more were installed between 1894 and 1905.

Prior to 1870, anyone could run a ferry as a private undertaking but after that date the new North-West Territorial Government began to receive complaints regarding the casual manner in which these private ferries were being operated. People who had travelled long distances were, at some point, faced with a ferry crossing. Often they were charged exorbitant tolls at the whim of the ferry owner or found the owner absent and the ferry not operating.

The North-West Territorial Government did its best to remedy this state of affairs and, as the ferry problem appears to have caused some concern right from the inception of the new government, it prepared the first Ferries Ordinance in 1877. After 1898, when the North-West Territorial Government's new Department of Public Works assumed responsibility for the ferries, it instigated a system under which ferry crossings were put up for competition, the man offering the highest bonus (to be paid to the government) receiving the licence to operate the ferry for a period of three years. This system, however, resulted in the levying of high tolls in order to make the venture a paying one for the ferryman and seriously taxed residents in certain areas where they had to use the ferry to reach their nearest market centre. The government then changed the system by paying a small monthly salary to ferrymen and, in addition, laying down a low schedule of tolls.

The Ferries Ordinance, which was revised from time to time, stipulated that ferries were to be operated at all hours of the day or night, seven days a week; between the hours of 9:00 p.m. and 6:00 a.m. double rates could be charged. All the ferries were operated under licence which cost $5.00 and granted the ferry operator/owner the exclusive right to such ferry during the period of the licence, usually for three years. The licence covered cable or "swing" ferries, which had to be of sufficient capacity to safely carry one double wagon loaded to 3,000 pounds capacity with two horses or other draught animals attached.

It was also specifically laid down in the Ferries Ordinance that children travelling to and from their schools were to be carried free of charge, and that "Her Majesty's mail shall in no case be obstructed."

A ferry was not to be used on any river or stream that was fordable at any time, nor could it block or injure such a ford. The ferryman was obliged to post on both sides of the river in a conspicuous place a schedule of ferry rates and hours of crossing, and to maintain a rowboat in case the water became too low for the ferry to operate. He was also obliged to maintain the approaches to the ferry in such condition that the ferry was reasonably accessible at all times for double loaded teams.

He was liable for all damages to persons and property resulting from carelessness on his part while using the ferry, but any person unlaw-

This ferry crossed the Bow River just above the barracks at Fort Calgary, not far from the present Centre Street bridge. It was photographed about 1884.

fully interfering with the ferryman's rights was liable to be convicted before a Justice of the Peace.

Any person using the ferry and refusing to pay the toll could expect the ferryman to lawfully seize his property then being ferried and could also be fined $50 or serve two months in prison. Likewise, if the ferryman injured or insulted any person, or damaged any property belonging to persons using the ferry, he faced a $100 fine and three months imprisonment.

Ferry inspectors travelled around the territory reporting on the condition of the ferries and on any infraction of the Ordinance.

The arrival of the railways in the 1880s and 1890s provided new bridges across the rivers at Edmonton, Calgary, Red Deer, Medicine Hat, Lethbridge, and Fort Macleod. However, these were railway bridges only in most cases and some ferries were retained to carry passengers across the rivers in these cities and towns until traffic and/or pedestrian bridges were built.

In 1898, the North-West Territorial Government was operating ferries at Victoria, Fort Saskatchewan, Medicine Hat, Blackfoot Crossing, Colles, and Tindastoll, with three private ferries crossing the Peace River road on the Pembina River (Belvedere), the Athabasca River (Fort Assiniboine), and across the narrows of Lesser

Slave Lake. The three latter ferries were all used extensively by travellers to the Yukon goldfields in 1898. However, by 1899, all ferries were under government jurisdiction, their system of reduced tolls giving much public satisfaction as it materially reduced the cost to people who were forced to use them.

In the early period, simple forms of power were sometimes used to operate ferries. One method was to run a rope through a hole at each end of a boat and pull it across the river by hand. In other instances, a crude flat raft was attached by a rope to a cable stretched across the river and pulled across by hand, such as a "farm ferry" used near Wainwright, Alberta. After settlers arrived, there were many such small, privately-owned ferries of all shapes and sizes, on farm and ranch lands, built and operated by farmers to enable them to cross smaller rivers and creeks on their own land.

Another form of ferry was created about 1907 or 1908, when the federal government's Inland Waters Directorate (Water Survey of Canada), began to build and install its own cable cars at selected points on rivers and streams for the purpose of sounding the water depths and flow, and to take sediment samples. Although these conveyances were not intended for public use, they were used at times for quick river crossings — a handy method of transportation, provided fingers were kept away from the overhead cable pulleys!

There were many other types of conveyances constructed and operated by local residents for their own purposes and convenience

The Fort Saskatchewan ferry, seen here, served local settlers, as well as the North-West Mounted Police. The barracks can be seen in the background of this 1890s view.

— a "bucket" ferry on the Belly River, not far from the McNeil store, and "plank" ferries which, if not always suitable for carrying passengers, at least provided a means of transporting supplies and equipment.

Many applications were received by the government over the years from people wishing to operate their own private ferries, and these were usually approved, providing that they were maintained for personal use only, operated at the owner's risk, and not used for public hire. In later years, permission had to be obtained from the federal Department of Lands & Forests for the operation of any private ferry.

The cable or current ferry was the type most commonly used on Alberta's rivers. This was the flat scow-type craft with a deck of 4x8 foot planks built across a base of keel joists. The earlier ferries came in a variety of sizes but after 1905 they were built more or less to standard specifications. All had some kind of hand rail along each side of the deck; most had wooden "aprons" at each end which could be lowered and raised to facilitate the loading and unloading. A high cable was stretched across the river between two cable towers, one on each side of the river, and on this ran the lead cable on two traveller pulleys attached to two steering pulleys down near the deck level, thence to the pilot wheel. This wheel, turned by the ferryman, angled the ferry into the river current, which set all the pulleys in motion. A current board which could be switched at an angle to catch the river current was fitted on the upstream side of the ferry, about twelve inches below the bottom of the ferry. On the return trip across the river this current board was again switched by a lever on deck to an angle which would catch the current again to take the ferry across.

The early cable and current ferries were hand operated by a ferryman turning the wheel on deck, but in later years gasoline motors were installed, making the ferryman's job a little easier. At crossings where the river was too wide for an overhead cable, or where the current was not strong enough, a small "pusher" motorboat was used to nudge the ferry back and forth across the river. Some ferries, indeed, remained man-powered as long as they were in service where river conditions did not warrant the help of a gasoline motor.

Cable ferries served Albertans through the years with very little modification of style and operation, although minor improvements have been made from time to time. A new design of apron hinge and keel strap were devised and fitted in the 1940s, and a new mooring device was designed in the 1950s. In the 1950s also, the guard rails along the sides of the ferry were painted black and white, which they still are today on the few remaining ferries.

II
Ferries in Alberta

In the late 1890s and early 1900s the North-West Territories were rapidly becoming populated. The Dominion Government, by its widespread advertising campaigns, was attracting immigrants from all over Europe and the United States. By the time the North-West Territories, already divided in 1882 into four provisional districts, were ready for provincial status, Alberta was fairly well settled around the large towns of Edmonton, Calgary, Red Deer, Medicine Hat and Lethbridge. All of these towns, their rivers spanned by bridges by 1905, had previously been served by ferries.

The new Alberta Government, formed in 1905, was composed mainly of newcomers to the West, and was quite unprepared for the mass migration which followed during its first few years. Thousands of people poured into what was still virtually an empty land — empty at least of proper roads and bridges, but intersected by the many rivers emanating from the Rocky Mountains watershed. The pioneer settlers were faced with the North and South Saskatchewan Rivers, the Bow, the Red Deer, the Athabasca, the Peace, the Pembina, the Big and Little Smoky Rivers, as well as smaller rivers such as the Wapiti, Baptiste (Berland), Beaver, McLeod, Oldman and Belly, few of which had been bridged or spanned by ferries.

The settlers were arriving at the railheads with all their worldly goods — household furniture, tools, implements, supplies and livestock — some with an old piano, organ or grandfather clock brought along with them to their new lives. From the railheads their long journeys to their chosen parts of the province were continued, using all manner of conveyance — wagons, carts, buckboards and prairie schooners, all hauled by horses, oxen and bulls. Shallow fords over coulees, sloughs and smaller rivers were crossed without too much difficulty as the pioneers, in most cases, followed trails already defined by earlier travellers who had found easy fording places at the rivers; but the wide, swifter flowing rivers presented real problems.

The only ferries existing in 1905 were the seven taken over by the Alberta government from the North-West Territorial Government — at Victoria (Pakan) and St. Paul (Brosseau) on the North Saskatchewan River; at Blackfoot Crossing on the Bow River; Steerford (Prin-

Bull teams of the American firm of I. G. Baker & Co. await their turn to cross the Oldman River near Fort Macleod about 1883. The ferry towers can be seen at centre.

ce's Ranch) on the Red Deer River; at Summerview on the Oldman River near Pincher Creek; the Belvedere ferry on the Pembina River, and the ferry (later Holmes' Crossing) on the Athabasca River near the ruins of the old Fort Assiniboine.

With limited funds at its disposal, the new provincial government was unable to meet all the urgent requests and petitions for bridges which were being received by the Department of Public Works in Edmonton. Instead they were obliged to respond to the demand by building and installing the relatively cheaper method of river crossing — the ferry — as a first means of meeting the settlers' requirements.

The 1905 season, as it happened, was extremely dry and, owing to very low water in most of the rivers, the existing ferries were maintained with some difficulty, but crossings could easily be made by fording the rivers. The government installed only one new ferry in 1905 — on the Red Deer River at the mouth of Tail Creek, where the little village of Content was located, and where the CPR line was then being built from Lacombe to Stettler.

To cope with the steady inflow of immigrants, four more ferries were built and installed by the provincial government in 1906; another four in 1907; and from then on the sounds of ferry building were heard at river crossings all over Alberta, culminating in a total of 77 government-operated ferries in the province by 1919. Unfortunately the ferry records for the first two decades of provincial administration are not available so the memories of pioneers and their families are about the only way of reconstructing the ferry history of that period.

The provincial Department of Public Works was originally responsible for the ferry system, as well as the roads and bridges. The Chief Public Works Engineer, J. D. Robertson was, during his term of office, in favour of a separate Ferry Branch but was unable to convince those in higher authority of its necessity. In the southern part of the province a full time ferry inspector, J. M. Farquharson, was employed during the early years, but in the central and northern districts the district engineer or district inspector supervised ferry operations.

One of the first engineers to be concerned with ferry operations was Jim Brookes. Brookes had come into the West as a member of an expedition travelling to the Yukon during the 1898 gold rush. They didn't reach the Yukon but he managed a couple of years panning for gold on the Finlay River in the vicinity of Fort St. John, making his way back to the Grande Prairie district, probably in the late fall of 1900. Brookes and other members of the expedition wintered at an old Beaver Indian camp known as the Lower Ford, just south of present-day Huallen. They built a log house with a chimney and stone fireplace, but during the long severe winter most of them developed scurvy and one man died. This came to be known in later years as the "Scurvy Camp."

In the spring the party built a boat and followed the river down to Peace River Crossing, and thence to Edmonton. According to Brookes' later report, he was the only surviving member of the original expedition. He was later employed by the provincial government and worked on ferries, roads and bridges in the Peace River country under District Engineer Alexander Hugh McQuarrie. He helped to put in the Peace River and Dunvegan ferries in 1908 and 1909, and in 1911 he built the first timber bridge at the site of the present city of Grande Prairie.

Brookes was also instrumental in the building and launching of about a dozen new ferries between 1905 and 1908 and it was he, together with a Captain Barber, who designed and built a power sweep to be used on the ferry at Peace River Crossing where the river and current were not suitable for the ordinary cable and current ferry.

Both Jim Brookes and McQuarrie, who joined the Department of Public Works in 1908, spent a good deal of their time tramping along river banks searching for ferry sites, where the current and also the approaches on each side of the river would be suitable.

As well as Brookes and McQuarrie, there were many other employees of the Department of Public Works who helped with the formation of the ferry system — men such as George Mills, Jim Gault, W.C.F. Beattie, Murray Cook, J. Farquharson, H. H. Forsyth, W. S. Playfair, John McBurnie, F. J. Graham, V. E. McCune, A. Hollas, N. McLean, W. Pallin, Walter Wanus, Jack Timblin, Bill and Howard Katherens and Al Dittman.

The surveys carried out by these early engineers and foremen were usually in response to petitions received from settlers where a new settlement required some method of river crossing. Such petitions were very popular, written on any handy piece of paper, scratchpaper or wrapping paper, signed by all the petitioners alongside their land location references. The engineers would survey the suggested ferry sites and present their recommendations to the Department of Public Works in Edmonton. Most of their travelling was done in the early model cars, on horseback or on foot, carrying tents, equipment and food with them. They camped in the bush or, if at a settlement or existing ferry crossing, a settler or the ferryman or his wife would cook them a meal.

Mail service already existed in the new province and its delivery, distribution and collection necessitated the appointment of mail carriers and the establishment of post offices. Very often the postmaster, if he was near a river crossing, would also operate the ferry. There was invariably some kind of habitation at or close to most river crossings — a settler's homestead, a stopping house, or a store — and any of the owners could have operated the ferry during the summer months in addition to tending their own operations.

Settlers bound for Grande Prairie cross the Peace River on the Dunvegan ferry during the teens.

23

These early ferrymen played an important and necessary role in the formation of the new province by assisting the incoming settlers to reach their chosen lands. Their struggles with the crude, current-operated scows against the ever-changing, unpredictable and untamed river currents, and their assistance with the loading and unloading and transportation of all kinds of settlers' effects on the river banks, are hard to imagine. Without these early ferries and ferrymen the map of Alberta, riven as it is from west to east by half a dozen major rivers and scores of smaller streams, may have presented quite a different pattern of settlement today. The early economy of the province, too, owes a great deal to these men, who later carried the farmers' grain and stock to railheads or to markets, and brought him back again with goods and supplies purchased with the proceeds of his sales. These early ferries were motivated entirely by manpower, the ferryman having to haul on the wheel to turn the ferry into the river current which carried it across; sometimes having to pike-pole the scow out from the river bank into the current, a task which often entailed enlisting the help of all passengers on board.

The installation of a new ferry called for all the necessary supplies of lumber, nails, tar, pitch and oakum to be assembled on the river bank near the proposed crossing. The ferry was usually built at the site and then launched into the river with the help of local residents, and perhaps a team of horses. On the North Saskatchewan River, many early ferries were built in Edmonton at John Walter's sawmill and boatbuilding yard, and floated up or down stream to the ferry sites.

John Walter's mill at Edmonton was one of the centres for building Alberta ferries.

24

The approaches to a proposed crossing, usually of earth which turned to gumbo during the spring rains, had to be graded and levelled. Some of these ferry approaches certainly added to the difficulties of river crossing when settlers' wagons and carts had to be extricated from the deep mud on both sides of the river.

A ferryman had to be appointed at each crossing for the summer season. This was a job eagerly sought after in the days when avenues of employment were scarce and certainly later during the Depression when jobs were almost non-existent. Government records still contain many pleading letters to the Department, to the premier, even to the prime minister, asking for jobs as ferrymen. Petitions were sent to the government, signed by members of a community who supported their choice of the man whom they felt would operate the ferry satisfactorily. A successful candidate was duly appointed before the river became navigable and if he was not a nearby farmer or postal official, a small shack was provided by the government where he could live at the crossing, often joined by his family during the ferry season.

Over the years, ferry service gradually became more organized and businesslike. The ferryman was required to sign a contract between himself and the ruling monarch (represented by the Minister of Public Works), signifying that he would operate the ferry at the place named in the contract in an efficient and orderly manner. The contract made the ferryman virtually the captain of his ship — responsible for the ferry, its equipment, the approaches, and of course the passengers and whatever was transported across the river. As the years went by, various time sheets and statistical forms were provided by the government so that the ferryman had a fair amount of paper work to do. Numbers and types of passengers, livestock, machinery, etc. had to be noted daily and later, when motorized vehicles replaced the horsedrawn wagons and buggies, the ferrymen kept supplies of waiver forms to be completed and signed by all drivers of heavy vehicles, accepting responsibility for any damage done to the ferry deck by the lugs on their wheels. These drivers were required to provide planks to protect the deck, or remove the lugs from the vehicle's wheels.

The ferries themselves gradually became equipped with pike poles, a shovel, pickaxe, jack, broom, first aid kit, axle grease, brushes, peavey, crowbar and oilcan, and the ferryman was also required to have a fire extinguisher, pump, cables, capstan, rubber knee and hip boots, skids and rollers and a little rowboat which was tied to the ferry and trailed in its wake on all its crossings. Supplies of pitch, oakum, tallow and coal tar were kept on hand in case repairs had to be made to the ferry during its operating season.

Each spring came the day, after the winter's ice had broken up and disappeared, when the ferryman decided that conditions were suitable for the ferry to make its first crossing of the season. It was launched, with the help of local residents, a local farmer loaning his team of horses, or later a tractor, to haul the ferry into the river. Immediately it was launched, the ferryman was required to send a telegram to the Department in Edmonton, advising them of the time and date of the ferry's first voyage. From then on the ferry was in business for the summer season, seven days a week, from 7:00 a.m. to 7:00 p.m., as a free ferry, a continuation of the provincial highway system, their locations appearing on provincial maps, and also on the road maps issued by the Rand-McNally company, who applied annually for ferry information.

From closing time at 7:00 p.m. to 7:00 a.m., the ferryman charged a small fee according to a schedule laid down by the Department, which payment was his to keep to supplement his salary and to recompense him in a small way for a disturbed night's sleep. Depending on the location of the crossing, the ferryman's summer could be a busy one, or travellers might be few and far between, but in either case he would make time for his other duties — his land, home, post office or store.

As captain of his small vessel he had the right to enforce the official regulations, some of which were that:

- all traffic has to board and leave the ferry on his instructions, and had to obey his orders regarding position on the ferry deck;
- he could refuse to carry any vehicle or load which appeared to be dangerous;
- he could refuse to operate the ferry at all if the river conditions made operation dangerous;
- if a team arrived first at the ferry it had the right of way and the ferryman could refuse to take any motor vehicle on the same trip in case it scared the horses. Likewise, a motor vehicle arriving at the ferry first had the right of way, and the team would have to wait.

These regulations are still in force today, with additional, more modern ones as to motor engines being shut off, brakes set, gears set in neutral. A chain was to be fastened across each end of the ferry so that vehicles would not roll off. This was sometimes overlooked and there were some instances of vehicles rolling off the ferry into the water, sometimes with fatal results. This brought about the regulation that all passengers must get out of their cars for the trip across, leaving their vehicles securely braked and geared into neutral, a regulation not necessary today.

As the ferry system grew to encompass most of the province, so, too, did the staff of ferry foremen, construction and maintenance

With the river filled with flowing ice, the Morrin ferry was pulled out for the winter.

crews. These men worked year round to ensure that all existing ferries were maintained in good condition, surveying new ferry sites, building new ferries, cable towers and small shacks as summer quarters for the ferrymen, even drilling water wells at some crossings for a supply of drinking water.

Winter conditions sometimes left the roads and ferry approaches in unusable condition, and these would have to be improved and re-graded in the spring. Laying gravel on the sticky gumbo was quite an innovation, but this sometimes had to be done in later years to provide a foundation in which vehicles would not become mired as they approached or left the ferry. The immediate approaches usually required a seven percent grade and to obtain this it was sometimes necessary to make the roads or trails leading to the ferry crossing about 1½ or two miles long — sometimes very winding, tortuous miles.

Early engineers and foremen such as George Mills, Jim Brookes and A. H. McQuarrie usually travelled alone but drew on staff from road or bridge crews for help when required; they also recruited the help of local residents for ferry building and repair.

Later engineers, such as Jack Timblin with his Pontiac coupe, and Bill Katherens with his McLaughlin Buick, formed the first "mobile ferry crews." They travelled with an 8' X 8' tent, a small oil drum for a heater, a pick and shovel, carpenter's tools, and two sets of eight inch block and tackle. The latter were indispensable for hauling themselves out of the muskeg which plagued the unwary traveller.

27

In the 1930s, ferry crews progressed to two larger 16' X 16' pyramid tents . . . and a camp cook! Only three names have come to light, Mrs. May Brown, a Mrs. Halversen, and Mrs. Lena Jeffreys, but there may have been more. Local history records show that Fred and Zena Popowich also worked with the ferry crews after the couple retired from their farm. Fred was also a former ferryman at Beauvallon.

The ferry crews travelled year round, camping in their tents even in winter, to ensure that the ferry system remained operable. Towards the end of the 1930s, the Department of Public Works provided trucks for travelling and employed a mobile crew of its own.

In the 1950s, the ferry crews had two bunkhouses and a cook car hauled by a truck, with the rest of the crew following in cars from crossing to crossing. During the summer and fall, the life of a ferry crew was unique and not unpleasant, travelling around the country-side, working in the open air all day and relaxing in camp after a hot meal in the evening.

Mrs. Lena Jeffrey of Drumheller worked for three years as a camp cook. Her first husband, Jim Smith, had been in charge of the Morrin ferry on the Red Deer River for over twenty years, and when the Morrin bridge was built in 1959 they both joined the ferry crew. Mrs. Jeffrey's memories of those years as a camp cook with the ferry crew tell the story:

> Bill Katherens persuaded my husband, Jim Smith, to join his ferry crew as a carpenter after the bridge was built at Morrin, and he also took the risk of hiring me as a cook. So we joined the outfit and began a new venture, not without misgivings on my part, and off we went in our little Austin car and caught up with the ferry crew at the Dorothy ferry.

> This was November 1959 and the countryside was very bleak . . . not too cheering an introduction to a new job. However, my part in it was comfortable enough — cooking for six or eight hungry men kept me both busy and warm in the cook car provided for the purpose. I don't recall what particular job they were doing at the Dorothy ferry that day, but working outside all day certainly made the men hungry. Busy as I was, catering to all these big appetites, I still found time to wander around the little hamlet of Dorothy in my spare time.

> The work to be done at each ferry crossing varied in time from days to weeks, depending on whether a new ferry or a new ferryman's house was required, or just minor repairs. When the job was completed, we travelled to the next assignment, which could be anywhere, from the next crossing on the same river, or way up at Fort Vermilion on the Peace River. I soon learned to pack the dishes, pots and pans, etc. so there would be no breakages during travelling. Country roads and the river hills leading down to crossings were usually very rough, and when steep inclines had to be negotiated, we were advised to remain on the opposite slope until the bunkhouse cars reached the top of the hill on the other side. There were two bunkhouses and a cook car. Jim and I travelled in our own car, of course, as did the other men in the ferry crew, and also the foreman, Mr. Katherens, if he happened to be with us. Since it was his job to inspect ferries throughout the province, and to decide what work was to be done at which crossings, he was only with the ferry crew periodically. Also, supplies had to be ordered and trucked in by

the truck which was used to move the bunkhouses to different locations, and this, too, was part of the foreman's job. One of the crew was in charge while the foreman was away, and, while I was working as the camp cook, Howard Katherens, Bill's brother, was in charge. They were both certainly very easy to work for. They got along well with the men and their sense of humour often made mealtimes very pleasant affairs.

Except for about a month, which included Christmas and New Year, the building and repair work on the ferries went on all through the year, no matter what the weather was like. Fires would have to be lit, sometimes, to thaw the ground to put in new "deadmen" or whatever was required and, needless to say, I had to keep a good supply of hot coffee at all times to give the men a chance to warm up for a few minutes now and again.

Some ferry locations were particularly isolated and even desolate, even in summer time — Finnegan and Jenner to name a couple — and the snow, ice and wind did nothing to enhance them. During one storm while we were at the Finnegan ferry, two of the crew lost their way coming from town and were not found until they were both badly frozen, one man losing part of both of his legs.

Weather conditions were the reason for the government providing us with a new cook car, which contained a long table where the men ate, a propane stove, a refrigerator, hot water tank and a cold water barrel. One end was curtained off as the cook's sleeping quarters. During the aforementioned storm, snow blew in through the door, through the windows and through every tiny crack, and the men had to brush the snow off the benches when they came in to eat. I wore two or three pairs of my husband's socks to keep my feet warm, and also sat on the hot water heater to keep warm.

Life never seemed humdrum while travelling with the ferry crew. We all enjoyed the work, and on holidays and at weekends when the men visited their homes, we were left free to explore our province and visit our children, who all lived in Edmonton at that time. We also had visits from friends who lived anywhere near a ferry location where we were at the time.

On one occasion a ferry had to be moved to another crossing downstream, so the scow was launched like a boat and off we sailed — about four of the crew, myself and enough food to last for the day. We drifted along with the current and the men rigged up a long pole to use as a rudder to keep the ferry in midstream and manoeuvre it into the bank at its new location. It was an interesting day and a long one, and we were happy to see the bunkhouses and cook car which had come by road to the new ferry location. We were all ready for a hot meal and a good night's sleep.

Another memorable voyage we took was in November, 1962. We were camped in the town of Peace River where the crew had built a new ferry which was to be taken to Fort Vermilion, 500 miles down the Peace River. More men were hired and my friend, Mabel, came to give me a hand with the cooking. The ferry at Fort Vermilion did not operate from an overhead cable, but was propelled by a tugboat; and great was the excitement when the new tugboat arrived by truck from Vancouver. Eventually we were ready for our journey from Peace River to Fort Vermilion, and the new ferry was loaded with the cook car, with plenty of food, tents for the men, Al Dittman's car, and a "wee house" which the crew had built especially for the trip (I think more for Mabel and I). Bill Katherens, retired by now, came along with us as he was still very interested in ferries and in the unique life connected with them that he had so much enjoyed.

There was quite a crowd to see us off and a reporter or two, and I can see a picture in my mind's eye now how we must have appeared — the little tug snugged up against the big ferry, making one wonder which was escorting which. No doubt

29

The ferry at Fort Vermilion is seen here in 1968. It had modern pontoons and was propelled across the wide Peace River by a pusher-type boat.

about it, though, the tugboat was in command, and under the bridge and down the river we went on our long voyage to Fort Vermilion.

The scenery was gorgeous and at times we saw the occasional deer on the river banks, and once a bear with two cubs watching us curiously. We startled a few trappers out of their solitude, too, bringing them down to the river's edge to call and wave to us. Even a whole family in one place — Ma and Pa and all the kids, laughing and waving excitedly. They wouldn't be seeing the likes of our river craft too often in that part of the world!

We put into "port" each night — a likely looking spot with a big tree nearby around which we could tie a stout rope attached to the ferry to stop it from drifting in the night, since we all had to sleep, even the pilot. I don't recall exactly how the men passed the time — played cards and swapped yarns, most likely, there being little or nothing for them to do otherwise. Mabel and I were busy with the meals and I was grateful for her help on this trip as I had broken a couple of ribs just before we left Peace River.

We put ashore briefly at the little settlement at Carcajou, which was really isolated, their only means of getting mail and supplies being by motorboat in the summer, and by dog sleigh in the winter. The men looked around the little village, and Mabel and I visited with the postmistress, then we were on our way again.

Bill Katherens became ill while we were travelling and Al Dittman took him by motorboat (fortunately part of the equipment on this trip) to where he could get to a doctor. I think we were three nights on the river, and the last stop before reaching the Fort was at Tompkins Landing (La Crete), where the ferry crossing was a wide one and the ferry was also operated by a tug instead of on an overhead cable. Here we saw a couple of farmers tackle the river with a couple of rafts loaded with farm machinery, heading downstream, trusting to their outboard motors . . . . and hope and faith!

30

It was here, too, that we took another pilot on board with his wife and family. Now there were eighteen of us, and Mabel and I were extremely busy in the cook car. There was no shortage of food, and we certainly had a very merry time.

At Fort Vermilion our trucks and bunkhouses awaited our arrival, as did all the local population. There were no dignitaries and no band, although I really think we merited one. Anyway, it was too muddy for ceremonies — we set up camp and got on with the work of settling the new ferry and tugboat into their new operation, and building a new house for the ferryman and his family. It had been a unique journey, experienced by only a few people.

Our roving life with the ferry crew didn't cut us off from our family, who came to see us when they knew where we were working. One time when my son, Jim, came to see us, he and I and a member of the ferry crew went for a walk, following a "cut line" through the bush — a daft thing to do because we got lost and were three mighty scared people before we finally found the river again. We had hopefully fired the rifle we had with us, but it might as well have been a peashooter for all the help it was.

I was in the habit of taking walks whenever I had the time, until we saw a bear swimming in the river one day, just above the ferry. After that, my daily outdoor exercise was limited to just around the camp!

Another anxious time for a nearby farm family was when their little four-year-old girl wandered off and got lost in the bush. A search was organized, and Al Dittman finally found her, perilously close to the river bank and a straight drop into the river.

My husband, Jim, thoroughly enjoyed our gypsy life with the ferry crew, too. He had served the public as ferryman at Morrin for over twenty years and had begun to find it rather trying. He enjoyed life with the ferry crew, doing the carpentering work and hauling water for the cook car and bunkhouses. The ferry crew themselves were a congenial lot, and we enjoyed the hospitality of many of their homes when we were in their vicinity.

Ferries that we worked on during my years as camp cook, besides the ones already mentioned, were Rosevear, Lac Ste. Anne, Wembley, Jenner, Fahler, Blue Ridge, Finnegan and Duchess — to name but a few. Some were in lovely surroundings, some were bleak and barren, most of them now replaced by bridges.

I enjoyed cooking for the men, and we enjoyed the travelling involved. The men weren't hard to please — at least there were never any complaints in the three years I cooked for them. I remember asking them how often they would like pancakes for breakfast. "Once a month" was the prompt and unanimous answer, which suited me very well since I didn't care for pancakes, either. The crew didn't criticize any of their former cooks at all, except to tell me of the cook who had served stew too often — about twice a day, in fact — so naturally I kept that good old standby to a minimum.

Living by the water all the time, it might be expected that we ate a lot of fish, but this was not the case. I don't think we ever had a meal of fish from the river but we did get a few while we were at Lac Ste. Anne, purchased, I believe, from the Indians who lived on the Alexis Indian Reserve on the other side of the lake. I drove, or sometimes walked, to nearby farms for eggs and cream in the summertime and always came away with fresh vegetables and sometimes an armful of flowers to brighten up the cook car. Indeed, quite often a box of fresh greens would be left at the camp and we would never know who the generous donors were. Also, I have always loved picking berries, and I made fresh blueberry and cranberry pies and shortcake when they grew where we camped.

31

Jim died in March, 1962, and although I stayed with the ferry crew until November, after our trip to Fort Vermilion I decided that my service as camp cook to the ferry crew was at an end. Both my husband and I, who were both employed by the Department of Highways, thoroughly enjoyed this very interesting phase of our lives.

At the first sign of ice in the river, the ferryman would prepare for winter and after operating the ferry for as long as possible, until solid ice formed, he would arrange to have the ferry hauled out of the water on skids and rollers and beached, high and dry, well out of the way of high water and large chunks of ice which were sometimes thrust up on to the river banks. He also was required to send a telegram to the Department, advising them of the time and date of the ferry's last trip.

There would then probably be a few anxious weeks when the ice was not strong enough to bear any weight, when mail and supplies could not reach the isolated community for which the ferry was a lifeline. The winter freeze-up and the spring break-up of the river ice were sometimes periods of real hardship and difficulty at some crossings, especially when there was no alternative route by the nearest bridge.

Depending on river conditions, its width and current, many different types of river crossings were devised at these times. In some instances a wooden plank was attached to the ferry cable and passengers would sit astride this and have a fast ride down the cable to its centre point; then would come the long, hard, hand-over-hand pull up the cable to the other side. At other crossings a slightly more elaborate, raft-like conveyance, with several planks nailed together, would be used. Whatever the type of crossing conveyance — some of them graced with names such as the "jigger" or "Go-Devil" — they managed to get urgent supplies and mail across the rivers to beleaguered communities. Travellers on these hair-raising rides usually had to climb up and down ladders attached to the cable towers on each side of the river.

In an emergency, an agile man could whip the bridle off his horse and sling it over the ferry cable, or use a clevis on a strap and maneouvre himself over, hanging on to the strap by hand; or sit in a loop of rope on the ferry cable and pull himself across.

There is also a recorded instance of a man "plank-walking" on the river ice. He carried two short planks, laying one down on the ice in front of him to cross in stages. What happened if he reached midstream and couldn't find a piece of firm ice is not recorded.

Another man tried to cross during a spring break-up by tying a rope around his waist with the other end tied to the overhead cable. He figured that he would cross on the cable, hand-over-hand, but, tiring halfway across, he let himself down to the end of his rope for a rest and then found that he couldn't pull himself up to the cable again. He dangled helplessly at the mercy of the cold wind with enormous chunks of ice rampaging down river just inches below him. Fortunately someone came along and saw his predicament and several lives were risked to get out and cut him down.

Sometimes a settler was faced with the prospect of a long journey of perhaps a hundred miles, of several days' duration, around to the nearest bridge when the ferry wasn't running. If he was within sight of his home across the river he might decide to take a chance and cross on the thin or slushy ice. Many lives and possessions were lost in that way.

As soon as winter conditions prevailed, various winter crossings were used, depending on the width, depth and current of the river. At some crossings the "cage" or "box", or whatever conveyance was used on the ferry cable, would be used all winter to carry mail, supplies, and the more hardy passenger. At other crossings, an ice "bridge" would be formed, either naturally or by pumping water on the ice to make a thicker, stronger roadway. These bridges were sometimes reinforced by logs, planks, river debris, etc., and the ferryman usually had a hand in preparing it for winter crossing. He would test the ice bridge daily until he decided that it was strong enough to bear the weight of all the winter traffic — teams and wagons, pedestrians, animals and, in later years, cars, trucks and buses.

A chinook or mild winter, however, precluded the use of the ice bridge by heavy traffic and its use would be limited to the hardy pedestrian brave enough to risk crossing on the unsafe ice. There are many stories of ice crossings. Mailmen, intent on getting the mail through, would tread gingerly on unstable ice, pulling or pushing their mail sacks along, or in a rowboat menaced by fast-moving chunks of ice. One intrepid lady store owner recalled crossing the river on her hands and knees, pushing the store cash box along on the ice in front of her.

Eventually the provincial government saw the necessity of providing and installing winter "cages" at some crossings — large, cage-type boxes, open so that the wind would not overturn them or impede their progress across the river — and eventually most of these were equipped with small gasoline motors to propel them. However, the open cages were hardly conducive to comfortable travel and passengers not only had a hair-raising ride but were liable to be lashed by icy winds blowing through the open cage as well.

Winter, spring and fall crossings were always an inconvenience. In earlier days there was absolutely no alternative method of crossing,

When the river was frozen over, an "ice bridge" made it possible for transportation to resume. Here, Fred Clegg's pigs wend their way across the Red Deer River at Morrin, on their way to market.

other than the ice bridge, the overhead conveyance, or a long journey around by the nearest bridge. Ferry users today are faced with the same problem at some crossings. Overhead conveyances are no more, but the ice bridge is still used, and, of course, modern cars make the detours to the nearest bridge much faster.

Efforts have been made over the years to combat the situation. In the late 1950s two companies offered the government equipment which had been developed to prevent ice formation. One method was a type of mesh gabion, a cylinder filled with stones such as is used in building dams and supporting bridge foundations; exactly how it was to be used at ferry crossings has not been established.

The other method was a "bubbler" system, with compressed air forced through a plastic pipe from the river bottom. Both systems were considered but turned down, as apparently there were no remaining ferry crossings with conditions suitable for either method. The "bubbler" system was offered to the provincial government again in the 1960s, but again rejected. However, the Saskatchewan government had installed this system at their Buffalo Narrows ferry crossing where a narrow strait connects two freshwater lakes. The channel at this site was 600 feet wide and fifty feet deep, with a sand base which prevented sub-cooling of the water at the bottom. The interchange of water between the two lakes provided a small current and a steady reservoir of warmer water at the bottom of the channel. A 600-foot loop of one inch diameter polyethylene hose was anchored by weights about ten feet below the water surface and connected to an air compressor which supplied air to the hose. The continuous bubbling action raised the lower warmer water to the surface, thereby keeping a 40-foot wide ice free channel across the Narrows, ensuring the operation of the 25 x 50 foot ferry on a year round basis.

In the 1970s, the Alberta government experimented with a hovercraft type ferry at Tompkin's Landing on the Peace River in the hope of keeping the crossing open all winter, with the ferry skimming over the surface of the ice, but after a couple of years it was decided that it was not a practical proposition. All were nice tries to beat the natural elements but proved that, after all, man is not the boss!

Although winter, spring and fall were always the seasons when crossings were difficult, there were many times when floods caused by heavy summer rainfall would hinder the ferry operation or dry periods of low water when the ferry was unable to operate. In the flood seasons the rivers, gathering force as they went along, would bring down all kinds of debris — trees, houses, barns. One time at a crossing, the floor of a barn was seen floating down river with two cows, placidly chewing their cuds, seemingly unperturbed by their wild ride; another time a hen house full of its cackling inhabitants, floated down. The larger debris sometimes caused ferries to break away from their cables, or broke the cable itself, and the ferry would join the downriver rush, sometimes alone, but once in a while with the ferryman and his passengers. One runaway ferry carried its frightened passengers along on a rough ride for about ten miles to the next ferry crossing where the ferryman had been alerted and, with a quickly mobilized gang of men, he hauled the runaway to safety. Another ferryman's wife had left her bread to rise in the kitchen when her husband called her to help to operate the ferry for one trip. The ferry broke away and went downriver with its load of passengers, and the sound of the ferryman's wife wailing, "my bread, my bread," wafting back to onlookers on the river bank.

The loss of a ferry through flood during the summer caused inconvenience and sometimes hardship to small communities who depended on the ferry to get to the grocery store for supplies and to the doctor. At these times, children were unable to cross to school, and social activities were also curtailed.

The uses to which ferries were put were quite varied. All of Alberta's ferries were, and are, free to travellers as continuations of the highway system where it was not possible or feasible to build a bridge. In the early part of the century before many bridges were built, the ferries were used by all manner of people and vehicles — incoming settlers with their wagons and teams, buggies, democrats, prairie schooners, livestock, household furniture and goods, and farmers with their hay wagons and loads of grain. In later years, there were automobiles, trucks, motorcycles, even a 10-ton caterpillar tractor at one crossing. At another crossing a whole house being moved to another location was taken across the river on a ferry.

Animals were also transported when farmers took their herds of cattle to summer grazing grounds. Many are the tales of cattle crossings, of the farmer and his men and the ferryman trying to coerce the lead cattle onto the ferry, to be followed by the rest of the herd swimming behind. Where the river was too deep or the current too strong, the herd would be ferried across in relays. On these occasions cows and their calves would become separated, resulting in much bawling by both mothers and babies; or else the whole herd would try to crowd onto the ferry at once, sometimes resulting in the sinking of the ferry and a thorough wetting for all concerned. On cattle crossing days the ferryman certainly earned his pay and he could look forward to the exercise being repeated when the herds were returned to their winter quarters in the fall. Sometimes frightened animals would jump off the ferry, to be followed by the rest of the herd, and large scale rescue operations had to be carried out before the crossing could be attempted once again.

Three thousand sheep were once crossed on a ferry, an operation which took many days, with sheep pens being built on each side of the river. As there is nothing more intractable and unintelligent than a sheep, one can imagine the problems on this particular occasion.

Herds of pigs, flocks of geese, turkeys and hens were all taken across on ferries, amid all the grunting, squawking, cackling and "cussing" that went on during these operations. In later years such livestock had to be suitably crated and controlled, but in the early days, they just had fun!

At one crossing, a beaver was said to have discovered the joys of ferry travel and rode back and forth several times; and one ferryman's pet gander kept him company, perched on the end of the ferry, performing his scratching and preening antics to the delight of the ferry passengers.

One rather nice aspect at some crossings was the use of the ferry as a gathering place for social evenings. Imagine a lovely summer evening, the deck of the ferry swept off for dancing to the music of the local fiddler and mouth organist, the river bank set up with tables of food prepared by the local ladies, young and old alike dancing on the ferry. Would-be travellers were taken across the river, but very often they would stay and join in the merriment. Corn roasts, potato roasts, barbecues and square dances were held "down at the ferry," with all comers welcome to join in.

One ferry was the site of an annual religious ceremony. The participants were baptized in the river, being "dunked" in the water from the end of the ferry.

Ferries also served as gossiping or meeting places, and Alberta ferrymen, whether they realized it or not, were at one time the hub of news and gossip for their whole area. Travellers from other villages, towns or a city would pass on news and the ferrymen would relay it to his family, friends and neighbours.

Ferries have been used, and probably still are, by doctors, school children, travelling salesmen, trappers, school teachers, police, government employees, mobile clinics, bus services, oil and lumber companies, and for carrying all kinds of supplies, mail, medicines, and equipment.

One particular use of the ferry which lingers in the memories of the early pioneers was for berry-picking expeditions. This important event usually took place on Sundays after church. At one time, wild berries were just about the only fruit available, so these outings, apart from being jolly family picnics, were necessary to ensure a supply of fruit for jams, jellies and pies.

Another use of ferries, or rather the ferryman, was by the federal Water Survey Board, which, if it required water soundings to be taken and recorded near a ferry crossing, would engage the services of the ferryman to do this job for them, paying him a small monthly remuneration for his services.

The Alberta Department of Public Works administered and maintained the ferry system from 1905 to 1951, when the Department of Highways was formed, later to become Alberta Transportation. These Departments and their employees — the surveyors, engineers, foremen, crews and administrative personnel — should not be forgotten. They all played an important role in the development of Alberta, assisting the ferrymen in their efforts to maintain the flow of traffic.

III
A Few Characters

All Alberta's ferrymen played their parts in history, but a few are singled out for specific mention. Some of them were not quite so bound by rules and conventions as they are today and were colourful characters.

Abraham Salvais (Battle River) will be remembered for his role as Louis Riel's compatriot in the 1885 Rebellion, and also as a freighter and buffalo hunter.

Morgan Buck (Belvedere) arrived from the United States about 1900, bringing with him an organ which is still in use at the Anglican church in Barrhead. He operated the Belvedere ferry for about eight years (1904-11), and was a real local character. Old Buck, or "Admiral" Buck, as he was called, used to walk around wearing a peaked cap, very much on his dignity as the operator of the small ferry. His cap apparently irked one man, who sat on the river bank one day and took a pot shot at it.

Basil Theroux (Brosseau) is recalled as an efficient and likeable ferry-man, a fun-loving, devil-may-care fellow, who was also known for his "home brew." He dispensed his moonshine to a few friends, which somehow became known to the RCMP. two strangers appeared one day and asked Basil if he knew where they could obtain something to "wet their whistles" and Basil replied, innocently, "Yes, but be sure not to tell the police or I will get into trouble." The two officers, dressed as civilians, obtained their bottle for which Basil charged them more than usual, and departed. When they were out of sight, they uncorked their bottle to taste the contents, which they found was nothing more than good old North Saskatchewan River water!

Joe Bissett (Dunvegan) walked into the Peace River area over the mountains by way of Prince George. It is said that he operated the ferry for the first few years it was in service, but sometimes he would get fed up with the job and want to quit. One day a disgruntled passenger told Joe that he would see that he lost his job, and Joe promptly offered to pay him $50 if he would get him fired. Another time, Ferry Inspector Jim Brookes, who did have the authority to fire Joe, was annoyed at being delayed and shouted to Joe to "bring the ferry across." Joe replied "go around if you are in a hurry." On another occasion, because of some miscalculation in docking the ferry, a settler's horse was drowned, but Joe didn't try to make any excuses. He paid for the horse there and then, and the settler made no complaint. Finally, Joe decided that he had had enough and, with his dog, he walked out of the area the way he came in.

A. J. "Alf" Monkman (Elk Point & Shandro) was a popular ferryman and is also remembered for his many years of service as a mailman. In spite of bad weather and almost impassable roads, he never failed to deliver the mail. For this, he was honoured by the people of Elk Point and district in 1928 by a banquet and the presentation of a gold watch. His wife, a lady of firm religious convictions, became convinced that the world would come to an end in 1919, and she had her husband and Bill Keller (also a ferryman), worked overtime to fill the woodshed. She never explained why they would need all that wood when the end of the world came, but laughed about her conviction later.

John Finnegan (Finnegan) will be remembered by his name on the map of Alberta, the Finnegan ferry being named after him. He came from Scotland in the 1880s and, a thin, wiry man, he was recalled by being able to turn hand springs at the age of seventy-five. His wife's flaky pastry, which she served in her boarding house to train crews, will also be remembered. Mrs. Finnegan was rather heavily built and some of the railroad men bet her that she couldn't get through a small attic door in her house. She tried, but got stuck and they had to help get her down.

Bobby Roberton (Forbesville) was recorded as a "most agreeable, affable, personable, kind and humorous man." He was married to a local Indian girl and, as the Rev. Albert D. Marshall said, "God gave them several smart and beautiful children" who endured the taunts of their schoolmates, such as "breeds" and "smoke" with the disdainful remark, "Oh, no! We're the improved Scots." One supercilious English passenger on the ferry once kidded Bobby by saying that while men of various nationalities married Indian girls, Englishmen seldom did. Bobby's instantaneous reply, in his soft, slow tone, was "Well, I guess the Indian girls have to draw the line somewhere."

Jasper "Buck" Smith (High River) was a one-eyed poker player who was called "The Man Who Never Misses" by the Blackfoot Indians

John Finnegan and his wife came from Scotland and settled at Finnegan, Alberta. Both were well known and popular throughout the district.

because he was the best shot in the territory. He settled in the High River area in 1878 and lived in a sod-roofed cabin, later building a large one and a half storey stopping house near the ford. He was a very hospitable man and often accommodated friends with free room and board. He was also an accomplished storyteller. "Why did I build a ferry on the river?" he once said. "Well, when I was crossing the river one spring during a flood, I was carried off downstream, out into the Bow River, then into the South Saskatchewan, and at last I floated ashore and met Sir John A. Macdonald. Sir John, hearing of my expeience, gave me the materials to build a ferry to see that people get safely across at High River."

George "Daddy" Houk came to southern Alberta in 1864 from Montana. He panned for gold in the Edmonton and Peace River areas, then returned south where he helped to build Fort Hamilton (re-named Fort Whoop-Up). He was one of the first ranchers on the east bank of the St. Mary River where, in addition to his ferry, he also ran a stopping house.

40

Louis Patenaude (Lea Park) was the first ferryman at Lea Park in 1908. He was remembered for having taken part in the Rebellion of 1885, and for saving the lives of two white women who were carried off by the Indians after the Frog Lake Massacre.

Nicholas Sheran (Lethbridge) was born in New York City, of Irish parentage. He had been a drummer boy with the Union Army when he was only fourteen and a member of a whaling crew in the Arctic before he came into southern Alberta looking for gold. He operated ferries at Fort Whoop-Up and at Coal Banks (Lethbridge), where he found rich coal deposits which opened up the area. Sheran was drowned in an accident at the Fort Kipp ferry in 1882.

J. S. "Jockie" Calder (Lunnford) had served as a scout in the Riel Rebellion of 1885 and was an interpreter at some of the Rebellion trials. He is said to have graduated from McGill University before settling as a homesteader and ferryman on the Pembina River. He was a master ferryman and knew how to deal with all river conditions — and he loved his pipe! He used to buy cheap tobacco which he blended with powdered red willow bark and drenched the mixture with perfume. He carried this in a beaded buckskin pouch attached to his belt, and when he filled and lit his pipe, people could smell the smoke from a mile away.

Andre (Andrew) Bleriot (Munson). According to his own memoirs, he left France in 1896 and, after working in various places in Canada, settled in the Munson area about 1901 or 1902. After returning to his native France to get married in 1910, he came back to his homestead where he "fixed a kind of ferry" and helped many early settlers to cross the river before the government ferry was installed in 1913. Bleriot's claim to fame is that, in 1909, his brother Louis, who had remained in France, became famous as the first man to fly across the English Channel in his own "lighter than air" flying machine.

Edward McNeil was never officially a ferryman but his rowboat "ferry" did transport passengers across the Belly River. He is remembered, not only as a genial and kindly storekeeper and family man, but also as an early farm instructor on the Blood Indian reserve. In 1896 he was shot in the hip by the Indian, Charcoal, who was later hunted by the police for the murder of Medicine Pipe Stem and Sergeant Wilde of the NWMP.

Colin Dick (Riverbow) was a veteran of World War One, a handsome, dapper man, always standing erect like a soldier awaiting inspection.

In addition to his postmaster and ferryman duties, he ran a taxi service with his Model T Ford. Colin fell in love in the mid-1930s and, as a result, his mail and post office duties were neglected. On several occasions it was impossible for anyone to make a phone call through the post office or to cross the river on the ferry, as Colin was away visiting his sweetheart.

Frank "Cougar" Wright (Sangudo), according to J. Bickersteth, "looked like (not acted like) St. Peter!" Frank came to Alberta from the United States about 1906 and homesteaded on the Pembina River, where he also ran the Sangudo ferry for many years. His home became a stopping place for travellers; he baked his own bread and pastries and also made very good sauerkraut. His son recalled that he was sometimes ill-tempered and "cranky as an old cougar," which gave him his nickname. Sometimes, before the ferry was installed, Frank would take a few drinks in the Sangudo hotel bar and return, somewhat shakily, on his hands and knees, across the railroad bridge.

Steven Hall (Steveville) gave his name to the district where the ferry crossed the Red Deer River, although the name has now disappeared from current maps. Mr. and Mrs. Hall ran the post office and a boarding house where their hospitality was famous and where everyone was welcome.

Ambrose Shaw (Steveville) came to Canada from England in a sailing ship in 1868 at the age of seven. He operated the Steveville ferry from 1912 until about 1930 and was always very friendly and helpful whatever time of the day or night anyone arrived at the ferry. He told one passenger that he always liked to eat a green apple at night before he went to bed.

IV
Individual Ferry Histories

The history of each individual ferry, appearing in the following pages, is provided in alphabetical order. Most of the land locations have been taken from either the Annual Reports of the Alberta government (hereinafter referred to as "annual reports") or from a list supplied by the government. In some cases, these locations appear to be the crossing where a ferry was finally installed after being moved from its original location. A few inconsistencies have been found, perhaps due to typographical errors. Other locations have been determined from local history books while the locations of some of the older ferries installed before 1905 have been derived from the Annual Reports of the North-West Territorial Government and from old maps on which established trails are marked.

To find the land location of NE21-59-12-5 (the north-east quarter of Section 21 on Range 59, Township 12, west of the 5th Meridian), look at a map of Alberta and find the 5th Meridian which runs south through Smith to Waterton Lakes. The Range numbers run north and south, Townships east and west. Find Range 59, move west to Township 12, which is marked in thirty-six sections. Count the sections starting from the bottom right hand section, east to west, back from west to east, and so on until Section 21 shows where the Allendale ferry was located.

ALLENDALE FERRY
(1915-53)
McLeod River   NE21-59-12-5

The Allendale district was named after David Allen, one of the first settlers west of the McLeod River; he lived about ten miles south-west of Whitecourt. He arrived in the area in 1908 and was soon followed by more settlers on both sides of the river.

By 1914, with many homesteads and farms well established, a link across the river was needed and requests were made for a ferry, particularly so that people on the west side could have access to Highway 32 then being built between Whitecourt and Peers. Accordingly, in the fall of 1914, Frank Chaisson, another early settler, was hired by the provincial government to "bring down the Athabasca

River a ferry which was to be placed on the McLeod River the next summer at a point to be decided upon by the provincial government."

The north-east quarter of homesteader George Ritchie's land was the chosen location, and on June 23, 1915, the ferry was launched with a champagne christening and named "The Peter Gunn," after one of the old chief factors of the Hudson's Bay Company. The *Whitecourt News* reported the ferry launching as "the greatest event of the season," followed by a picnic, games, and free rides on the ferry for the rest of the day. George Ritchie, the first ferryman, performed the honours as captain.

The ferry service continued for thirty-nine years, with Paul Linehan as the next ferryman, serving from 1915 to 1935. Paul's wife was the woman who left her bread to rise when she was called to help him with the ferry. When it broke away, she went off downriver, more worried about her bread than the runaway ferry.

AMETHYST FERRY
(1912-20)
Bow River   14-18-18-4

This ferry was first installed as "Kinnondale," which was a post settlement about twenty-five miles south of Bassano, perhaps named after early postmaster, J. C. McKinnon. The name of the post settlement was changed to Amethyst in 1917.

AMISK LAKE FERRY
(ca. 1940)
East of Boyle

This privately built and operated ferry plied across Amisk Lake in the 1940s. It was used only by two families, the Arndts and the Hartleys, to save long journeys around the lake. Government records of 1940 indicate the existence of this ferry, but there is no information as to what type it was or how long it was in operation.

ANTONSEN'S FERRY
(1926-?)
Pembina River

There was a ford at this location in the early 1900s, as well as at the Sunniebend (Adair's) Crossing a few miles down-river. When the community of Sunniebend decided to build a bridge in 1921, the Sunniebend ferry was discontinued. The little timber bridge carried traffic across the river until 1925, when high flood waters carried it away. A ferry was installed on the river on Carl Antonsen's land in 1926 and operated during that summer. However, Antonsen wanted the ferry to remain and in 1927 he petitioned the government for its retention. He indicated that if it were discontinued the twenty-two people across the river would either have to cross in a rowboat, which he said was too dangerous, or walk six miles to the store for their mail and supplies. According to the annual report, the ferry did remain at Antonsen's Crossing for the 1927 season, where it was operated by the public themselves. It was not listed in subsequent annual reports, but the government sent supplies of tar, pitch and oakum to the site in 1928 for the usual spring repairs, so it may have continued to operate until the bridge at Sunniebend opened in 1931.

ATHABASCA LANDING FERRY
(1906-51)
Athabasca River

The Athabasca Landing area was used both as a landing and a crossing as far back as the late 18th century. The Hudson's Bay Company built a post there to which supplies were freighted from Edmonton for distribution to other forts and houses. The Landing also saw many travellers through the ensuing years — missionaries, railway and geological surveyors, North-West Mounted Police, as well as hundreds of "Klondikers" who passed through the area in 1898, followed by thousands of emigrating settlers on their way to the Peace River and Grande Prairie districts. Settlement at the Landing began in

The Athabasca ferry is seen here in the 1930s.

1888 and by 1911, when it was incorporated as the Town of Athabasca Landing, it boasted a population of 800. The "Landing" was dropped by ministerial order on August 4, 1913, when it became known as "Athabasca."

With an increasing influx of settlers after the turn of the century, the provincial government installed a ferry in 1906, prior to which the river had to be forded. The ferry operated for 46 years until the bridge was built in 1951, and was apparently a very busy one as it was the only means of access to the country north of the river for many miles. The railway reached Athabasca from Edmonton in 1912 and farmers and trappers came in from the north, using the ferry to transport their crops and furs to the railhead.

Crossings were made on the river ice in winter, but in 1934 a "cage" was installed on the ferry cable for spring and autumn use. Passengers for the "cage" would tie up their horses and sleigh dogs on the north bank to await their return. Bill Katherens recalled that, on occasion, live pigs, sheep, turkeys and chickens were also taken across in the "cage," which also carried all the mail brought in by post officials of northern settlements for the Athabasca post office. Mrs. Daisy Gooding recalled one post official, a rather stout lady, who arrived at the ferry one day in spring when the ferry wasn't running because of river ice. Mrs. Gooding's father, Christopher Johnson, the ferryman at the time, was taking people across in a canoe, but he refused to take the stout lady and her mailbag. Finally the mailbag was taken to the post office by the ferryman's other daughter, an eleven-year-old girl. However, the postmaster refused to accept the mail from an "unauthorized person," and accompanied the girl back to the crossing where, after seeing the very stout postmistress, he decided to forget the matter and accepted the mailbag.

ATLEE FERRY
(1916-61)
Red Deer River   NS2-23-7-4

This ferry was installed on the Red Deer River about seven miles north of the Atlee settlement to enable farmers north of the river to haul their grain to the railway. Located near the Magnus Bjork ranch, it apparently served its purposes faithfully but uneventfully for about forty-five years. All that remains today are the old wooden foundations of the ferryman's house.

The ferry must have had a flurry of activity for two years as it was designated as a Class A ferry in 1929, requiring the services of two ferrymen, and a new scow was built in 1930. However, it returned to a Class B ferry (one ferryman) again in 1931.

46

BANFF FERRY
(1884-86?)
Bow River

When the Canadian Pacific Railway reached Siding 29 (Banff), it erected a section house and David Keefe and his wife (reputedly the first white woman in the area) built a small hotel nearby.

The lower hot springs (the present Cave & Basin) had been discovered in 1883 by the McCardell brothers and Frank McCabe; Keefe, realizing the potential value of the hot springs as a tourist attraction, constructed a crude ferry across the river to them. He used CPR ties for the raft-type ferry, tied together with CPR wire. Another length of wire was strung across the river to which the raft was attached, enabling early tourists and travellers to pull themselves back and forth across the river to the spring. The river, although deep at this point, had no appreciable current and the crossing was quite a safe one.

In 1886, D. B. Woodworth, the enterprising politician from Nova Scotia, claimed to have purchased the hot springs from McCabe and the McCardells, and he applied to the North-West Territorial Government for a licence to operate a cable ferry across the Bow River at Banff. He purchased materials and engaged labour to build a road from the river to the hot spring, but the government decided to construct a floating bridge to replace Keefe's crude ferry.

BASSANO FERRY
(1914—?)
Bow River   N½-31-19-18-4

This ferry shown as being installed in 1914 "S. of Bassano," was operated by the public at their own convenience. Its location was on McKinnon's XL Ranch and was known locally as McKinnon's Crossing. It appears on the annual reports for 1914, 1915 and 1916, but not for 1917. Listed again in 1918 and 1919, when a new scow was built, it apparently continued to be operated by the public as it appears again on the 1924 annual report.

BATTLE RIVER FERRIES
(1885-1909?)

In 1885 a little party of geological surveyors travelled down the Battle River by canoe from the Calgary-Edmonton Trail, among them eighteen-year-old Henry Tyrrell, who recorded the journey. He mentioned passing through two "little half-breed settlements," the first being Todd's Crossing, south of present-day Gwynne, where Donald Todd, a veteran buffalo hunter and trader had settled with some half dozen families who depended on fishing as a livelihood. There was no

The Ferry Point ferry is one of several which operated along the Battle River. This view was taken about 1903-05.

mention of a ferry at this crossing where the river was probably shallow enough to ford. Salvais' Crossing was a few miles further down river where Abraham Salvais (Salois, Solway), an active participant in the Riel Rebellion at Batoche, had settled earlier to carry on his buffalo hunting and freighting activities. Henry Tyrrell recorded that Salvais was apparently in the Edmonton Gaol at the time the surveying party went through, accounting for his actions at Batoche, but Salvais did, in fact, own and operate a ferry at this crossing — probably the first ferry on the Battle River.

The Battle River valley saw many subsequent travellers en route from Battleford to Wetaskiwin, and many early settlers came in over the trails from the east, many of whom chose their homesteads in the lush, green valley.

At Ferry Point, the first homesteaders had been settling in since 1897, and in 1902, traders George and Norman Smith of Duhamel engaged Bob Mutch to assemble a load of lumber on the Pipestone Creek at Gwynne and float it down the Battle River, through Dried Meat Lake, to the Ferry Point site. Here, with the help of neighbouring settlers, a store was built and operated by the Smith brothers. After the store was finished, the Smith brothers had a barge built at Duhamel, loaded it with merchandise, and floated it down river to Ferry Point. This barge was then used as a ferry. In 1903, when the store was sold to Thomas Thirsk, Ferry Point consisted of the store, a post office and the ferry, but by 1905 the population of the area had increased to the point where the little ferry was overworked, so a small steel bridge was built.

As the valley became even more populated after 1905, the provincial government installed a ferry in 1907 at a location shown in the annual report as "South Vermilion." In 1909, this ferry was "moved to a point

48

The ferry which spanned the Battle River near Hardisty is seen here in 1909, about two years after it was established.

over the Battle River at 19-45-7-4," according to the annual report, which is close to present-day Fabyan. Also in 1909 another ferry was installed "North of Chauvin" at 23-45-2-4, but neither ferry appears in the 1910 annual report. In the meantime, ca. 1907, a ferry had been built and launched at Hardisty. The Hardisty Town Council paid for the materials and construction of this ferry, which was built in the Allen Johnstone lumber yard, then loaded on to a stoneboat and hauled down to the river. It was launched with the help of Will Siebrasse and his team of horses, Kit and Ned. Al Jeglum and Noah McCombs were the first ferrymen. Hiram Brody Wood, always known as "H.B.", later took over as ferryman until the traffic bridge was built.

This little ferry was kept very busy in 1907 and 1908, carrying many settlers and their goods across the river to their homesteads southeast of the town. "H.B." Wood, who slept and cooked his meals in a tent by the river, charged 25 cents for a load and ten cents for a single foot passenger. The ferry was attached to a cable and pulled across the river by hand and, on arrival on the opposite side, a crank was turned to lock the ferry into place while it was unloaded and loaded again. It was usually left on the ferryman's side of the river when not in use and would-be passengers from across the river had to shout for service.

Another little private ferry on the Battle River was built and operated some time in the early 1900s by Ralph Smith, who discovered coal in the vicinity of Donalda. His ferry was used by people who wanted to

49

get across the river for coal. The name of the little post settlement of Fairybank (36-43-27-4) on the Battle River was changed to Ferrybank in 1905. They may also have had a ferry there before the bridge was built in 1907.

BEAUVALLON FERRY
(1932-58)
North Saskatchewan River   14-55-10-4

The little settlement of Beauvallon on the CPR line about seven miles south of the river was incorporated in 1909, all the land on the north side of the river being settled in the ensuing years. Although the Myrnam ferry, installed in 1914 some seven or eight miles to the east, served as a crossing for some of the settlers, petitions for a ferry north of Beauvallon were started about 1917. These came from settlers north of the river, backed up by requests from the Municipal Districts of Sobor and Champlain, as well as the Beauvallon Board of Trade. In order to get their grain to the railhead and purchase supplies at Beauvallon, farmers and residents had to travel many miles around to the Myrnam or Brosseau ferries, or ford the river when possible, at the rapids just west of where the ferry was later located. However, the years went by with continued but fruitless petitions for a ferry.

There was some controversy amongst the various petitioners as to the site but by 1920 all parties were agreed on a location suitable to all. However, it was not until 1931, when the Brosseau bridge was opened to traffic, that the government agreed to the old Brosseau ferry and the ferryman's house being moved to the Beauvallon Crossing. After thirteen years of petitioning, the cable towers were built, roads and approaches upgraded, and the Beauvallon ferry was launched on September 17, 1932.

These were the Depression years and many applications and petitions were received for the position of ferryman. Moise Donie was appointed as the first ferryman, but in 1933, the government inadvertently appointed two different ferrymen, Moise Donie and Wasyl Zawalinsky. This caused a little friction, but Moise Donie got the job again and remained as the ferryman for a further fourteen years.

During the summer months the ferry was kept busy hauling grain and supplies, not to mention the usual berry picking and picnic trips during leisure hours. Winter crossings were made on the ice, with a "cage" installed on the high cable for spring and fall crossings. This was hand-operated and used in emergencies only. The ferry apparently gave good service for twenty-six years, no reports of accidents or mishaps being recorded. It remained as a Class B ferry (single operator) during its years of operation and, according to oldtimers in the area, it was never fitted with a gasoline motor, the rapid flow of water at this point being sufficient to operate it by the current boards.

In the 1950s, with a community grazing pasture in use south of the river, there was no need to transport herds of cattle across the river. Some of the smaller access roads were not being used and were closed, and traffic on the ferry gradually decreased.

The spring of 1956 saw unusually large amounts of ice, some in chunks 25 feet high, blocking the launching of the ferry, and a lot of work and money was expended in clearing it away. This left the approaches in such poor condition that District Engineer A. N. Coulter recommended that the ferry be discontinued and in 1958 it was floated down to the Myrnam crossing to replace the old scow there.

BEAVER CREEK FERRY
(1902-?)
Beaverhill Lake

Joseph McCallum, an early settler who had arrived in the Vegreville area in the spring of 1891, built and operated a private ferry in 1902 on Beaver Creek north of the lake, probably where the old North-West Mounted Police trail crossed, and somewhere in the vicinity of the present bridge on Highway 16.

The *Edmonton Bulletin* of June 13, 1902 reported that ". . . we are informed that Joseph McCallum intends putting a ferry on the creek soon . . ." and on 27 June 1902 it had a further note ". . . the ferry on Beaver Creek is working well. Charge for teams is .50¢."

No further references to this ferry have been found and it is not known how long it was in operation.

BEAVER CROSSING FERRY
(1911-20)
Beaver River   15-62-2-4

This location, formerly Cold Lake, had its name changed to Beaver Crossing in 1913. The missionaries came into the area as early as 1844, the mission at Le Goff being established in 1849. A Hudson's Bay Company post, too, was in operation 1885, situated on the west shore of Cold Lake, and the ford across the river, south of today's Grand Centre, was used by many travellers, early settlers and the North-West Mounted Police.

As the railway did not reach St. Paul until 1920, early settlers had to haul their grain all the way to Vegreville, the road to Vermilion having many steep hills along the way.

The area was fairly well settled by 1911 and the provincial government installed a ferry in that year to shorten the journey for people living north of the river. The ferry, located about 100 yards below the present bridge, operated from 6:00 am to 6:00 pm daily, with Albert Limoges as the first ferryman. The only other known ferryman was Joseph "Grandpa" Dery who, as well as being an efficient ferryman from about 1916 to 1918, was also handy as a dentist, a barber, a carpenter and furniture maker.

Although no incidents or accidents connected with the ferry itself have come to light, there are several stories of crossing when the ferry was not operating. The Poirier brothers used to cross by means of a clevis on a rope slung over the ferry cable. Charlie Demeriez, not to be outdone, felt that if the Poiriers went across this way, then he could, too, but when he tried it, hanging from the cable with his bare hands, he fell into the river and had to swim to safety.

Another early pioneer, Fred Hebert, arrived at the crossing one evening and, failing to get the ferryman's attention, climbed the cable tower, crossed the cable hand over hand, and brought the ferry across to where his wagon and oxen were waiting.

The ferry was discontinued when a bridge was built in 1920.

BELVEDERE FERRY
(1898-1911)
Pembina River   1/36-58-3-5

Also known as Pembina Crossing and MacDonald's Crossing this site was named for Belvedere, Kent, England, and was located on the old Hudson's Bay Company pack trail from Edmonton to Fort Assiniboine. In 1898 the old trail saw thousands of gold-hungry "Klondikers" on their way to the gold fields, and in that year a private ferry was built and operated by one Johnny Foley. It operated under licence of the North-West Territorial Government who described the ferry as "being used only by freighters and persons travelling into the north country, and not a public conveyance for the purpose of giving settlers access to the market." The schedule of tolls was high but was no doubt gladly paid by people travelling on the Klondike Trail.

There were not many settlers in the area in 1896, but Gordon MacDonald and his wife arrived from England in that year and kept a trading post and stopping house at the crossing. More settlers began to arrive about 1900 from which date MacDonald's Crossing, as it was then known, was changed to Belvedere.

In 1900, also, Morgan Buck arrived at Belvedere from the United States and homesteaded near the river. In 1904, he took over the operation of the ferry from Johnny Foley, a job which he retained until the ferry was discontinued in 1911. "Admiral" Buck, as he was known locally, used to walk around wearing a peaked cap, very much on his dignity as ferry captain. On one occasion when several people were waiting for the ferry to be launched after the spring break-up, they saw the "Admiral" get into his rowboat, row out to the centre of the river, grip both sides of the boat with his hands and put his feet up in the air. By this strange method he must have decided that the time was ripe for the ferry to be launched, as he rowed back to the north bank and arranged for the ferry to be put into the water.

In 1910, the Rev. Oswin Leighton, son of the Bishop of London, England, travelled across on the Belvedere ferry and was impressed with the community which he described as "quite a metropolis — the very fine, fifty-yard wide river with thickly wooded banks, a store and a stopping house."

Between 1900 and 1914, the area became more settled and populous, and at one time seventeen district post offices received their mail through Belvedere. A bridge was opened to traffic in 1912, when ferry service was abandoned and the ferry floated down to a new point west of Edson.

BERRYMOOR FERRY
(1916-83)
North Saskatchewan River   SE14-50-6-5

The Berrymoor post office was established in 1910. According to some sources, it was named because of the many wild berry patches in the area, although some oldtimers think it may have been named for early settler Martin Berry, a lumberjack who worked for John Walter in Edmonton before World War One.

The river had to be forded in summer and crossed on the ice in winter, but by 1915 there was enough crossing traffic to warrant the installation of a ferry. The provincial government installed one in the spring of 1916, listing its location as "South of Tomahawk" and almost immediately it was carried away by a spring flood. A replacement ferry then had to be floated down from Rocky Mountain House.

Winter crossings were made via an ice bridge if the weather was cold enough, otherwise travellers were obliged to make the longer journey around by the Genesee or Drayton Valley bridges. Bill Katherens, the provincial government ferry foreman, reported in his memoirs that:

> The water at this crossing was the fastest of any crossing we had to deal with . . .
> On one occasion, while we were doing some work there in the early spring, the ice was still strong enough to walk on so we packed our tools across on foot. A few days later when the job was completed, we fixed up a hand sled to pull the tools back across to our camp. Just as we stepped off the ice on the other side, we heard a roar behind us — the ice had broken and in a few moments there was none left. We had missed disaster by just a few seconds.

The Bleriot ferry was an important link across the Red Deer River. It is seen here in 1928.

The ferry was in operation for 66 years and was used quite extensively throughout that period. Bert Laiss, the last ferryman, said that many people drove miles out of their way just to cross on the ferry. People used it to visit the recreation areas in the district and, as in early days, it was still used by people going on berry-picking expeditions. The new bridge, ready in the fall of 1983, was looked forward to by only half of the local residents — many of them would have liked the ferry to remain.

The first Berrymoor ferryman in 1916 was Frank Lewis, who ran the ferry for several years; he was followed (date unknown) by Bob Fitzgerald, who lived in his own little shack not far from the ferry crossing. Local history tells of Bob being found shot to death one day, his rifle by his side, and it was assumed that it had discharged while he was cleaning it. According to the story, Bob was buried in a homemade coffin on the hillside overlooking the river and many years later, when a road crew was working on the grade to the river, Bob's body was disinterred and reburied elsewhere. The Rev. James M. Plank is listed as the ferryman in 1925; he apparently alternated his ferryman's duties with his religious activities. From 1926 to 1946, George Crocombe, a very well-liked and kindly man, operated the ferry.

BIG ISLAND FERRY
(1907-16, 1948-51)
North Saskatchewan River

According to the annual reports, a ferry was installed in 1907 as "West of Ellerslie", about two miles north of Big Island (3-52-25-4). In 1908 another location was listed about two miles south of Big Island (north of 20-21-25-4). As the government reported only the Big Island ferry until 1915, it is assumed that the ferry was moved for the 1908 season. The report indicates that this ferry was "replaced by a bridge in 1916" although which bridge replaced it is not clear.

The residents of Stony Plain, especially the farmers, petitioned the government in 1916 for a ferry just north of Big Island (33-51-25-4) because they "were cut off in winter," and they said that they would help to build the approach roads if the government provided a ferry. The petition, however, was turned down.

In 1948, after the Imperial Leduc No. 1 well hit oil and the company town of Devon was built, the government put in a ferry where the present bridge on Highway 60 crosses the river. It was listed as the Woodbend ferry and operated for only two years until the bridge was opened to traffic in 1951.

BIG ISLAND FERRY
Belly River

To get across the river from the Anglican mission, founded in 1880 by the Rev. Samuel Trivett, on Big Island, NW of Standoff, to the Indian Agency on the east bank, a little "boat ferry" was used during the summer, often in conditions made treacherous by high water and floods. Winter crossings could be made on the ice. The mission was inhabited until 1923, but there is no record of how long the little "boat ferry" operated.

BINDLOSS FERRY (1956-61)
South Saskatchewan River   SE27-19-2-4

In October 1941 the Bindloss UFA asked the provincial government to put a ferry at the above location because the British Block (CFB Suffield) had cut off their direct road to Medicine Hat, leaving them with many extra miles to travel around the Block. The government, although it promised to investigate the possibility of a ferry being put in that same winter, apparently rejected the request.

However, community efforts continued for the next fifteen years to find a shorter route to Medicine Hat, and a ferry was finally built and put into service in 1956. The launching was attended by Highways

Minister Gordon Taylor, local MLA Harry Strom, Bob Crawford, the Highways District Engineer, and officials from the Medicine Hat Chamber of Commerce, the happy day being marked by a picnic supper on the riverbank at the ferry crossing.

The ferry operated for six years until the Sandy Point bridge was opened to traffic in 1961.

BLACKFOOT RESERVE FERRIES
(1882-?)
Bow River

The first recorded ferry in this area was built at the Blackfoot Crossing in 1882 by the North-West Mounted Police. Captain C. E. Denny reported that he had, in that year:

> . . . a ferry boat ready built at Blackfoot Crossing, and I am awaiting instructions as to how it will be run. It would be well to keep it in the hands of the department, letting it on shares, the rent to go to the Indians.

Although the Indians had always used the crossing by fording the river, it was, in fact, quite a difficult crossing, especially for the police with their wagons and military equipment. Although no further reference to this early ferry has been found, it is presumed that it remained in operation for several years. Although local history records a ferry being built about 1890, known as the "Yellow Horse" ferry, the North-West Territorial Government reports make no mention of one until their 1899 report, which states:

> . . . the ferry across the Bow River at the Blackfoot Crossing was established during the past year [1899]. This stream is not of a fordable nature and for a considerable period of the year the water is at that stage and the current so rapid that crossing, even by means of a ferry, is difficult.

The ferry, under licence of the North-West Territorial Government, was listed in all subsequent annual reports until it was taken over by the provincial government in 1905. However, in the 1903 report of the North-West Territorial Government, they indicate that the ferry was moved from Blackfoot Crossing:

> . . . some trouble and inconvenience was occasioned by the ferry over the Bow River at the Blackfoot Reserve breaking away and being carried downstream. This ferry was established at a point known as Eagle Ribs, about seven or eight miles above the location of the old ferry, this point being selected at the request of the settlers.

The new provincial government built a new ferry for Eagle Ribs Crossing in 1906, but it broke away from its cable in 1908 and went off

56

downriver, apparently never being recovered. Local residents wanted the replacement to be installed further east, but the new one, built at the site, was put on the river at the same location. This was also known locally as the "Dick Bad Boy" ferry. While this was being built, travellers used the temporary ferry provided for crews building the bridge north of Arrowwood. In 1909, the latter ferry was moved to a point near the South Mission School where it is listed in the annual reports until 1912.

Oldtimers recall another time when the ferry broke away when Doctor Holmes and his car were on board. The ferry was caught and hauled back, but the doctor lost his car, with all his medical equipment in it.

A wooden bridge was built south of Cluny in 1917, which was the year that two ferries were in use at this point, one apparently to serve the bridge crews operating for that year only. However, the ferry at "S. of Cluny" was listed in the annual reports for another seven years — until 1924.

As the area south of the Indian reserve became more populated and farmers east of Arrowwood found it to be a long haul around by the Arrowwood bridge, they asked the government for a ferry directly south of Gleichen. The farmers all agreed to put up the sum of $1,000 between them and were all prepared to build and operate a ferry themselves, so the government finally installed one on Sec 12-21-23-4, about three miles east of the bridge, which is listed in 1923 and 1924 only. Travel over this ferry necessitated permission being obtained to cross the reserve to get to Gleichen, and also the erection of a small bridge over the irrigation ditch. This, the Arrowwood Ferry, operated for only a short time as the railway went through Arrowwood about 1926 and farmers did not need to travel to Gleichen with their grain.

In 1923 a new ferry was built and installed just south of Crowfoot, where it still operates today. It is used by Indian families, oil drilling employees, and by many tourists from all parts of the world, being so close to the Trans-Canada Highway.

BLAKELEY FERRY
(ca. 1951—?)
Peace River

When Frank Blakeley, his father, and two brothers took up land on the east side of Peace River in 1951 to extend their holdings on the west side, near Grimshaw, there was no way for them to cross the river so they built their own ferry. The distance from the Blakeley farmhouse on the west side to their land across on the east is eight miles as the crow flies. But to get to it by the existing highways and bridges they would have had to travel north to the town of Peace River where they would cross on the town bridge, then head south and west for sixty miles, cross the Smoky River at the Watino bridge and then travel north again to reach their farmland — a distance of more than 100 miles.

The Blakeleys continued to operate their ferry, which they called "The Homesteader," and which was propelled by a powerful D8 Cat motor. It carried four cars, and during the summer Mr. Blakeley crossed on his ferry almost every day, carrying farm machinery back and forth between his two farms. Other farmers who owned land on both sides of the river called on Mr. Blakeley if they wanted to cross and people who lived on the east side who wanted to get to Peace River town relied on "The Homesteader" to get them across. Mr. Blakely charged $5.00 if he was crossing anyway, but $10.00 if he had to make a special trip. One year, the family took the ferry sixty miles downriver to Dunvegan for Mackenzie Days, with the Beaverlodge Band playing on its deck.

There have also been a number of mishaps. Once the engine seized up and the ferry floated five miles downriver before Mr. Blakeley could get it started again. Another time someone cut the rope by which the ferry was moored and it ended up on a sand bar a few miles away. One year, when the ice piled up in the spring, "The Homesteader" got pushed up a tree!

A bulldozer kept the approaches in good shape, but the Blakeleys and other families in the area were happy when the provincial government installed the Shaftesbury ferry on June 17, 1977.

BLERIOT FERRY
(1913-present)
Red Deer River   W½-15-30-21-4

Although this ferry was installed in 1913 as "West of Munson" and listed by that name officially until 1966, its name was changed to honour its first ferrymen, early settler Andre Bleriot. He was a brother of the world-famous aviator, Louis Bleriot, the first man to fly across the English Channel from France in a "lighter-than-air" flying machine in 1909.

Andre (Andrew) Bleriot settled on a flat on the Red Deer River about 1901 or 1902, according to his own story. He told of returning to France in 1910 to marry, and, after his return to the Munson area, he "fixed a kind of ferry which was later taken over by the government." He carried many early travellers and settlers across the river on his own ferry, and also on the government ferry on which he was the first

A load of hay was taken across the river by the Bleriot ferry in the early 1920s.

ferryman. Bleriot served in France during World War One, then returned to his homestead for a few years, finally settling in his homeland in 1925.

The government ferry carried hundreds of settlers, their families, tons of settlers' effects, machinery, livestock, etc. In 1913 it carried over 1,200 vehicles, and over 23,000 in 1978. It remains in operation, still used by local farmers and residents, but is also a tourist attraction on the circular Dinosaur Trail from Drumheller. It operated for over forty years as a ferry powered by the river current, but a motor was installed in 1958 to enable it to cope with the increased traffic.

BLUE RIDGE FERRY
(1919-77)
Athabasca River   SW2-60-10-5

The little settlement of Blue Ridge was established about 1920 when the railway was being built through from Edmonton to Whitecourt. John Watson erected a store at Lonira, south of the railway, and opened a rough trail to the station and track area to the north-east. Because the district was covered with blueberries that summer, he called the little settlement Blue Ridge.

The government had installed a ferry in 1919, listed as "North of Greencourt" by which name it appeared in the annual reports until 1923. In 1924 the name was changed on the reports to "Christmas Creek" until 1927 when it appeared as "Blue Ridge."

The early crossing actually had two ferries as the site had a small island in midstream. Traffic had to disembark from one ferry and embark on the other at the opposite side of the island. The ferryman had a shack on each side of the river so that he could stay at either one, depending on which side of the river he was on at nightfall.

Bill Katherens, the government Ferry Inspector (1936-1960) recalled one time when the ferry crew were working at Blue Ridge:

> We camped on the midstream island one winter while giving the ferry a major overhaul. We built four new towers, making them much higher than before, and replaced both high line cables. Our camp consisted of two 16' x 16' pyramid tents, one being occupied by the cook, Mrs. May Brown, the other by the crew. It was customary for one of the crew to stoke up the fire in the night, but one night it went out and the cook had to light it again in the morning, which didn't please her very much. That morning my false teeth were frozen in a mug of water and the only way to thaw them out was on the cook stove — which didn't improve the cook's temper at all!
>
> The following summer I visited the island again and found all the camp debris we had left there the previous year hanging 15 feet up in the trees. The ice which had formed that winter had caused the water to back up and flood the island, leaving the debris high up in the branches.
>
> A few years later we built a new crossing a little upstream where only one ferry was required.
>
> The water here was extremely fast — crossing in the overhead cage during a spring breakup was really a thrilling ride. The ice would run wild below us with an occasional large ice cake turning on edge and bumping the bottom of the cage in which we were riding. When the water receded there were hundreds of acres of the low lands covered with cakes of ice, some of them four feet thick.

According to government records there was apparently another ferry further west on the Athabasca at 1-60-11-5 between the Blue Ridge ferry and Whitecourt, although the dates of its operation are not recorded. Perhaps this was the "Payne ferry" which was apparently about four miles upriver from the Blue Ridge crossing.

The Blue Ridge ferry remained in operation until 1977, used mostly by farmers and local residents, although oil company employees used it from time to time. It also carried many tourists who sometimes drove miles out of their way to experience this now novel way of river crossing. The cage was not used during the last years of the ferry's operation, an ice bridge being marked out for people who wished to cross it at their own risk.

BOW ISLAND FERRY
(1908-68)
South Saskatchewan River   E15-11-11-4 & SW17-11-11-4

The 1908 annual report indicated that "the ferry operated heretofore at Medicine Hat has not been required on account of completion of a

The ferrymen's grandchildren, Bertina and Inger Anderson, found the Bow Island craft excellent for fishing in 1924. The ferryman, Andrew Anderson, is at the rear in the light hat.

bridge there, and was moved up river to a point near Bow Island and operated there during the season."

Until 1911, the old ferry served people travelling to Brooks and Vauxhall, and children crossing the river to school. In that year, a new ferry was built. A total of six ferries were used at this crossing — three built at the crossing, three towed in from other crossings.

Winter crossings were made on an ice bridge and in spring and fall, a "bucket" or "basket" was installed on the ferry cable, and the ferrymen took people across in this in real emergencies. One story tells of three men who fell to their deaths in the fast flowing icy river in 1919 while riding in the "bucket." However, there are conflicting reports as to their mode of travel, whether it was the "bucket" or a boat.

During the summer months, the ferry was free from 7:00 am until midnight, after which there were charges of 25 cents for a car, 20 cents for a horse and rider, and 10 cents for every horse, mule, ox, cow, sheep or hog without a vehicle. One local rancher is said to have used the ferry to move 5,000 sheep across the river, three hundred at a time. This was done during the day, naturally, when the ferry was free, otherwise it would have cost him about $500.

When the ferry was ready to start its 1931 summer season, enormous chunks of ice and debris had to be removed from the river before the craft could be launched. Conditions in that year also hampered the movement of herds of antelope which, for many years, had used this area to cross the river to their summer grazing grounds. They were seen trying to cross at several different places along the

61

river but apparently managed a crossing further east towards Medicine Hat.

The ferry crossing was moved to its second location, about two miles up river, close to the present bridge, in 1943, where it continued in operation until 1968.

On one occasion in the late 1950s, the ferry almost sank with about 35 head of cattle on board, but they all got ashore safely, and the partly submerged ferry was hauled back to the riverbank.

It was used extensively during the 1950s and 1960s — not only was it the only means of crossing the river, but hundreds of people used it on weekends to make pleasure trips into the countryside. The last ferryman, John Hoel, took as many as 4,000 people and about 1,500 cars across one summer, not to mention trucks, tractors, motorcycles, horses, cattle, sheep, and pigs.

Although the ferry served residents of the area faithfully for sixty years, they happily attended the opening of the modern, six-pier bridge in 1968, celebrating the event with a barbeque luncheon and games on the river bank.

BOWSLOPE FERRY
(1918-58)
Bow River   SE¼1-15-16-4

Although local farmers had petitioned the government for a bridge at this point to enable them to reach the railways at Vauxhall and Brooks, a ferry was built and installed in 1918 after local settler, J. A. Hawkinson, agreed to act as ferryman. However, this was not always a satisfactory method of crossing. A 1922 petition for a bridge stated that

> the farmers in the territory are under a severe handicap in marketing their farm produce, by reason of the fact that the ferry cannot be operated at low water in the fall, when the ferry is most needed.

However, they had to manage with the ferry for another thirty-six years. It was replaced at least three times during its forty years of operation, in 1935, 1946, and again in 1955 when a larger scow was built to accommodate the increased traffic flow. Every spring the ferry was repaired, weak timbers replaced, new aprons built and fresh pitch and caulking applied.

An ice bridge was used for winter crossings, and no crossings could be made at all during the spring and fall river conditions. On one occasion, an irate hunter demanded to be taken across when ice made the ferry crossing impossible; the ferryman finally had to take a pot

Ferryman Basil Theroux is seen taking a load across the North Saskatchewan River on the Brosseau ferry in 1912.

shot at him to scare him off. Another accident, recalled by oldtimers, is when Mrs. Isberg's car brakes failed as she was driving off the ferry. The car plunged into deep water and floated off until it came to rest on a mud flat, where Mrs. Isberg managed to open the car window and put her baby daughter on top of the car until they were rescued an hour later.

Construction of the long-awaited bridge started in 1957, and although an ice jam and resulting floods washed away part of the construction early in 1958, the bridge was opened to traffic in October of that year and the old ferry was towed down to Empress for a few more years service there.

BREMNER'S CROSSING
Red Deer River   13-38-26-4

A petition was submitted by the Red Deer Board of Trade in January 1919 for a ferry to be installed at the above crossing, approximately nine miles north of Red Deer at a sharp bend in the river. Local farmers who wanted marketing facilities were cut off from Red Deer and compelled to travel about fifteen miles to reach a small village and about twenty-two miles to the nearest town (Red Deer). The petition was turned down and there is no record to indicate if the ferry was ever built.

BROSSEAU FERRY

(1907-30)

North Saskatchewan River

The ferry which had operated as "St. Paul," under licence of the North-West Territorial Government since 1900, remained in service at the crossing until 1907 when the Alberta Government built and installed its own ferry. Edmond Brosseau had arrived at the crossing in 1904, opened a store and started a horse ranch and fur trading business. The settlement became known as "Brosseau," by which name the ferry was listed in the annual reports until 1918. It reverted to "St. Paul" from 1919 to 1923, and was listed again as "Brosseau" from 1920 until 1930, its last year of operation.

In the early days, grain had to be hauled about eighty miles to the nearest elevators, a journey of several days' travel with slow-moving oxen, but the ferry shortened the distance somewhat. It carried many teams of oxen and horses, and many motor vehicles in later years.

Winter crossings were made on an ice bridge, and Joe Dubuc told the story of the late fall of 1915 when a threshing outfit was required at Brosseau to thresh the grain waiting in the barns. The owners of the heavy threshing outfit decided that the ice was not strong enough to carry its weight, so they found a licensed steam engineer, one George Lambert, who agreed to build a stronger ice bridge. For two weeks

Even when their days were numbered, ferries continued to provide service. Here, the Brosseau ferry remained active during bridge construction in 1930.

Lambert piled straw, tree branches and debris across the thin ice, spraying it every night with water pumped out from beneath the ice. When he finally pronounced his bridge to be ready, a large crowd assembled on the river bank to watch the steam tractor and threshing outfit creak and puff its way across. When it reached the north bank safely, Lambert, attired in a big fur coat and black Derby hat, bowed to the watching crowd, took a swig from a crock of whiskey he carried in his pocket, and drove off in a neighbour's sleigh.

A 1929 survey showed that 35,000 vehicles crossed on the ferry during that year. Oldtimers recall that the ferryman that year refused to carry a moving van containing all Dr. Lebell's furniture en route from Edmonton to Brosseau. The furniture all had to be unpacked, loaded onto the ferry, and re-packed onto trucks on the other side.

Also in 1929, a sad accident claimed the life of local farmer, Ferdinand Lord, who backed his car off the ferry and was drowned, leaving a wife and several young children. This accident prompted local residents, the Board of Trade, and young parish priest, Father Doyle, to petition the government for a bridge. It was built the following year and opened to traffic in 1931. The Rev. Monsignor Charles Hugo Doyle, now of Peekskill, New York, recalls their petition which resulted in the bridge being built.

However, Basil Theroux, the popular ferryman, may also have played a part in getting the bridge built. In 1928, when traffic waited in a line-up for hours to get across on the ferry, Premier Brownlee had wanted to move to the head of the line, and Basil had told him, in no uncertain tones, that everyone, even a premier, had to wait his turn. At the same time he pointed out the need for a bridge. According to local tradition, Basil was relieved of his job a short while after his little altercation with the premier. However, he probably smiled to himself when, shortly after his dismissal, the ferry cable broke and the ferry floated off downriver for about six miles. After 1931, while traffic crossed the river on the new steel and concrete bridge, the old ferry lay forgotten and rotting on the river bank.

BUFFALO CROSSING FERRY
(1914-30)
Red Deer River   W½10-22-6-4

Installed as "N. of Buffalo" in 1914, this ferry was not listed in the annual reports of 1916 to 1918 or 1923. The name was changed to Buffalo Crossing in 1924, and it was listed in the annual reports until 1930. No information has been found regarding its thirteen years of service between the Atlee and Pancras (Cavendish) ferries.

CALGARY FERRIES
(1877-93)
Bow and Elbow Rivers

When the North-West Mounted Police arrived at the site of the future city of Calgary in 1875 they found the Bow River to be a quite formidable barrier and had to find some means of crossing with their guns and military equipment. There were several shallow fords, one just west of today's Langevin Bridge, one at the present Cushing Bridge site, and the other about a hundred yards east of the Louise Bridge. The police were obliged to use temporary rafts and wagons with the wheels removed to effect a crossing.

In 1877, police accounts show that they "paid H. Paquette . . . $50 for building a ferry boat for the Bow River." This, possibly one of the earliest ferries in the area, may have been the police ferry recalled by oldtimers in later years as the "white ferry," used by the police to transport their cricket teams across the river.

In 1882, Fogg's Ferry was installed on the Bow, just about where today's Centre Street bridge stands. In 1883, after the railway arrived and with many more travellers and supplies for the north to be transported across the river, a new ferry was built. In March, 1883, the *Medicine Hat News* reported that

> work on the Calgary ferry is being pushed forward with vigour so as to have it in running order by the opening of navigation. The ferry is to be a first class one, the boat being 70 X 20 feet, capable of crossing six loaded wagons on one trip. It is to be situated at the other end of the lower bottom and will be an immense boon to travellers from the east as it will shorten the road from Medicine Hat some 2 or 3 miles, and save a difficult, dangerous and oft-times impassable ford.

(The "lower bottom" was the stretch of river bank from today's Centre Street to the confluence of the Bow and Elbow Rivers, just east of the fort, where the trail from Blackfoot Crossing and Medicine Hat dropped downhill into the little townsite east of the Elbow.)

The *Calgary Herald*, also in 1883, called for an appropriation of public funds to built a Bow River bridge "over this highway of commerce to the north," and in 1886-87, the Eau Claire Company built the Bowmarsh Bridge, just west of today's Louise Bridge. This carried some of the northbound traffic, as also did the Centre Street bridge built in 1887. However, the Bow River ferry continued to operate until the Langevin Bridge was built in 1890.

Two more ferries were installed in 1891, one from the fort area across to St. George's Island which had just opened to Calgary citizens as a park; and another east of the townsite "near the iron bridge near Mr. Rivers' residence" in today's Valleyfield district. This ferry "opened up another pleasant drive out into the country" for Calgary residents.

Also, a small rowboat ferry carried passengers across the Bow River to the sanitarium at Bowness, probably some time before the 1920s, and a privately-owned cable ferry plied across in the present Point McKay area to transport workers and equipment across to the brick works at the little district of Brickburn.

In addition to the Bow River, a number of ferries operated on the Elbow. The earliest reference was on August 6, 1884, when the *Calgary Herald* reported:

> A ferry boat is being placed on the Elbow River just below the railway bridge. This is a necessity, as fording the stream is unpleasant and the approach to it on the east side is very bad on account of the high hill. The boat is to be 30 feet long and 12 feet wide. Messrs. Jarrett and Cushing have the contract for the work and expect to have everything ready tomorrow.

A week later, on August 13, the *Herald* added:

> the ferry on the Elbow is at work at last and, owing to the low prices charged, a great number take advantage of it instead of using the ford, which at present is about the worst on the Elbow. The rates each way are .20¢ for a double rig; .10¢ for a single rig or a saddle horse; and .05¢ for foot passengers.

Another ferry operated across the Elbow also, about 1890, in the present Erlton vicinity. This was attached to a cable and had to be pulled across; frequently it had to be retrieved from downriver when the cable broke. It was used to transport funerals across to the cemetery — the coffin and minister first, followed by the pallbearers and mourners. This ferry operated until a bridge was built in 1893.

CANMORE FERRY
(1887-92)
Bow River

A seam of coal was discovered in the Canmore area in 1884 by Frank McCabe and the McCardell brothers, but a mine was not opened until 1887, when a ferry was installed to transport miners and coal across the river. A corduroy bridge was built in 1892 to replace the ferry.

CARCAJOU FERRY
Peace River

This is, or was, a privately owned and operated ferry on the Keg River Metis Settlement, halfway between Manning and High Level. It is not known how long it was there or whether it is still in use. The only information on it was related by Al Dittman, the former Ferry Inspector of the provincial government, who said that he was once ferried across the river at this point, one evening just about sundown, with the sound of the Metis ferryman's song remaining in his memory as a particularly pleasant few minutes.

CARSELAND FERRY
1908-20
Bow River   NE¼-21-25-4

Prior to 1908 early settlers crossed the river in summer at two fords, one upriver one downriver from the present bridge. In winter they crossed where thick ice formed.

The government installed a ferry in 1908 about half a mile downriver from the present bridge. However, as gravel bars formed over the years, making the ferry operation impossible, it was moved in 1915 to a crossing a short distance upriver. The road into Wyndham Park now runs over the early ferry trail. The ferry carried two four-horse wagons loaded with grain or loads of similar weight, but during periods of low water only one team and wagon could be transported, sometimes resulting in long lines of teams and wagons waiting to cross on the ferry, which worked continuously all through the day to get them all across.

Travellers still used an ice bridge in winter. On one occasion a local doctor crossed on the ice bridge in his car, standing on the running board and steering the car with one hand, ready to jump if the ice gave way.

The Carseland bridge was opened to traffic in 1920 when the ferry was discontinued.

CASH CITY (Proposed ferry)
(ca. 1890)
Red Deer River

Lewis Martin Sage opened a small store and post office on the west bank of the river, just west of Innisfail, in 1890 and purchased the McKenzie Ferry with a view to operating it at his new settlement, Cash City. Sage was so optimistic about his proposed ferry service that he composed the following verse in readiness:

> It will be arranged that, upon pulling a string
> A bell will ring
> Which will cause the ferryman to quickly spring,
> And you to the other side he will bring,
> And as he rakes in the tin, with cheerful voice will sing

However, the manager of the lumber company on the opposite side of the river, with whom Sage had been feuding, refused to grant him landing rights, so his proposed ferry service never materialized.

CHIN FERRY
(1920-22)
Oldman River   31-10-18-4

The 1920 annual report states "new ferry installed N. of Chin on the Oldman River." The ferry operated for three years only.

CLOVER BAR FERRY
(1883-1904)
North Saskatchewan River

Although a Church of England Mission had been established at Clover Bar in 1877, there is no indication that a ferry was in use in those early days. *The Commercial* of Sept. 18, 1883, reported that

a new ferry is being arranged at Clover Bar which will be run by a cable between there and Hermitage. The Edmonton & Saskatchewan Land Company is about to erect the buildings at Clover Bar and supply the cable for the ferry.

In the Edmonton ferry history, it will be noted that John Walter installed a ferry in 1883 where the Clover Bar bridge crosses the river.

A report in the *1885 Rebellion — The Alberta Field Force,* indicates that General Strange stated that

A ferry in use at Clover, with wire cable, was purchased and taken along so that if required the cable could be stretched across the river and a cable swing ferry operated to transfer troops across the river.

However, a ferry was in use after the rebellion as Charles F. Stewart was granted a license as ferryman for the period 1889 to 1892, and probably longer. The ferry was still listed in the North-West Territorial Government reports for 1902 and 1904. It was also active in 1905 as the first report of the provincial government indicated that the old Clover Bar ferry was floated down to Victoria (Pakan), where it was used in 1905 and 1906.

COALDALE FERRY
(1910-13)
Oldman River   26/35-10-20-4

In 1902, Thomas Patrick Nolan, with his wife, four children, all their household goods — plus a cat and four kittens — started life on their ranch on the north bank of the Oldman River, north of the present

The Coaldale ferry was known locally as Nolan's ferry because of its operator, Thomas Patrick Nolan.

town of Coaldale. Shortly afterwards, Mr. Nolan built and operated his own ferry so that he and other local farmers could cross to Coaldale and the railway.

The provincial government made no mention of the Nolan ferry in 1905, but installed a government ferry in 1910 as "N. of Coaldale" at the above location. This was in service until a bridge was built in 1913 — a new bridge, the Nolan Bridge, being built in 1967. In the 1914 annual report, the N. of Coaldale ferry was "moved to Grand Forks" *(see Grassy Lake)*.

COLLES FERRY
(1898)
St. Mary's River

H.J.C. Colles, reputedly a remittance man, took over the old Alexander & Clark stopping house about 1889 at the ford on the St. Mary's River, about ten miles south of Cardston, just north of present-day Kimball. Colles was also the postmaster and Colles, as a district, is listed in the 1898 directory as a post office and stopping place.

The river at that point was fordable with the aid of a guide, even during the spring run-off periods, but Colles operated a ferry there in 1898, probably collecting fees from gold-seekers on their way to the Yukon goldfields. It operated under license of the North-West Territorial Government and was only listed by them in 1898.

CONTENT FERRY
(1905-06)
Red Deer River

The area which was once the site of the old Tail Creek settlement, the winter camp of the Metis buffalo hunters, attracted many early settlers around the turn of the century. Among them was Arthur Content who had previously operated a stopping house near Innisfail. He settled on the west bank of the river and the little village of Content quickly grew, with a lumber mill, a creamery, and several stores. Settlers west of the river crossed by means of a rowboat ferry operated by a man named Kramer, who is remembered as being very reliable and helpful.

In 1905, the provincial government installed "a new ferry at the mouth of Tail Creek" but this only operated for two years as the Content bridge was built in 1906. The Content ferry was then floated downriver to "a point east of Olds" where it was put into service at the old Tolman Crossing.

One local resident recalled an exciting afternoon when the Content ferry cable broke as he, his wife and small daughter were crossing. Fortunately the cable was held by a splice clamp but the ferry swung around with its side against the bank so that they were unable to drive off. The side rails had to be removed and the gap between the ferry and the bank filled in with logs, brush and dirt so that the team could be taken off, fortunately on their home side. They then used the rowboat to cross to the store for supplies and left the ferry to be returned to its crossing by the ferry repair crew.

When the railway line between Stettler and Lacombe passed by a few miles to the north, the little village of Content disappeared. One by one its buildings were moved away or torn down until it was no more.

COSMO FERRY
(1912-15)
Pembina River   13-57-6-5

Local history recalls that the Cosmo ferry, located just west of the Whittome & Ford store in Cosmo, was installed in 1912 but it appears in the annual ferry reports for 1913, 1914 and 1915 only. However, a 1912 photograph shows the first trip of the Cosmo ferry, a gala occasion and the scene of some jubilation. The ferry disappeared from the annual reports in 1916, but in that year another ferry was reported on the Pembina River, as "N. of Sangudo" "where the range line crosses the river," which would put it at about 6-57-6-5. Research has shown that the Pembina River ferries were moved about quite frequently, and with no records available, it is impossible to follow their movements with complete accuracy.

COWLEY FERRY
(ca. 1898)

Among the early settlers in the Cowley area were LaFontaine and Bouthillier, the latter at the ford on the river where, in times of high water, he ran the ferry. A bridge was built across the Middle Fork, below Cowley, in 1899.

CROOKED LAKE FERRY
(early 1900s)

In the early 1900s, when the Gwynne valley was being settled, pioneer settler Adolph Rupertus built a raft and operated a ferry service across the south end of the lake. He did a booming business transporting travellers, teams and wagons across.

The Rupertus homestead was half a mile from Gwynne, on SW30-46-22-4, but it is not known whether the ferry was also at this location.

CROOKED RAPIDS FERRY
(1896-1900)
North Saskatchewan River

In the North-West Mounted Police report for 1896, Supt. A. H. Griesbach refers to

> . . . a ferry at Crooked Rapids. This was built during the winter and put into running order last spring. The owner of this scow, Amable Paradis, was given assistance by the Indian Department, the North West Government and the Police. The placing of this ferry at the point where it was operated has been the means of opening up a splendid farming country, viz., that part situated between Egg (Whitford) Lake and Saddle Lake, by means of a good trail, and also shortens the distance from Saddle Lake to Edmonton by 30 miles.

In 1900, the North-West Territorial Government stated that

> . . . at Paradis Crossing of the North Saskatchewan the ferry is owned by private parties, but a small bonus was paid towards its operation last season as there was not enough ferriage to justify the owner devoting his whole time to the operation without a bonus.

The above reports tell the story of this old ferry, which was not included in the annual reports after 1900, when it is assumed that it was discontinued. However, in 1901, the *Edmonton Bulletin* (7 June), reported that ". . . a new ferry, operated by the Saddle Lake Indian Agency, is now operating about five miles below Paradis."

The location of Crooked Rapids has not been located on any maps, but it was probably on the river bend east of Victoria (Pakan), an assumption borne out by the fact that "five miles below Paradis" would be the location of the ferry taken over by the province in 1905 as "East of Whitford" — later Desjarlais.

DESJARLAIS FERRY
(1901-1910-1962)
North Saskatchewan River   11-57-14-4

The 1901 annual report of the North-West Territorial Government stated:

> we arranged . . . in conjunction with the Indian Department, to operate a ferry on the North Saskatchewan River at Saddle Lake. We provided for use there a cable which had been used at Victoria . . . and some blocks and outfit from the old ferry at Fort Pitt, and the Indian Department undertook to provide the scow and operate the ferry.

A year later (June 7, 1901) the *Edmonton Bulletin* confirmed that "a new ferry, operated by the Saddle Lake Indian Agency, is now operating about five miles below Paradis." These two reports presumably deal with the ferry which later became known as the Desjarlais ferry, probably named after David Desjarlais, the postmaster and owner of a general store at the little settlement of Desjarlais. Not much is known about the operation of the early ferry, but it is assumed that it was necessary for the Indians from the Saddle Lake Reserve to cross the river, and for settlers to reach the railway.

It apparently operated under its old N.W. Territorial Government licence until 1909, as the provincial government did not put in its own ferry until the 1910 season. In that year it noted in its annual report that "a licensed ferry was operated East of Whitford."

Two of the early ferrymen, Fred and Alex Melnychuk, were reported by Bill Katherens (Government Ferry Inspector, 1936-1960) to have "only two legs and three hands between them." Alex had lost a hand while operating a power machine and Fred lost both legs while working as a CPR brakeman. They were, however, apparently efficient ferrymen. Only two recorded accidents have been found connected with the ferry. In 1936, little Lena Shapka fell off while it was crossing and, after an extensive search, her body was found two weeks later about two miles east of Duvernay. In 1944, a man left his truck in reverse gear and when he started it up to disembark, it backed off the ferry and the man was drowned.

The old ferry was sold by tender in 1962 when the bridge was opened to traffic.

DOROTHY FERRY

(1906-75)
Red Deer River   SE4-27-17-4

The little village of Dorothy was not even in existence when a ferry was installed in 1906 "N. of Gleichen." Hundreds of early settlers left the railway at Gleichen or Bassano and crossed the river on the ferry, bringing with them all their worldly goods, including livestock. They came with ox and horse teams and wagons, sometimes both a cow and a horse making up a team, and as many of them never thought about bringing any axle grease along, there were many squeaking wagons wheels by the time the crossing was reached.

Dorothy was incorporated as a post office in 1908, named after Dorothy Wilson, the first and only baby in the district at that time. Percy McBeath ran the post office and a general store (where he kept good supplies of axle grease), and also acted as ferryman when the ferry was moved nearer to his store, about 1908. McBeath was the ferryman from 1908 until 1916, when he moved away, but he helped many more settlers to ferry across, sometimes working late into the night to move their outfits across the river. One of his biggest ferrying jobs, which took about three days, was the long line of carts and mules on their way to build a section of railway line.

The ladies of Dorothy held quilting bees, and many ladies from across the river crossed on the ferry to attend these. The Blackfoot Indians, too, were ferried across with their haying equipment. One day an Indian baby died and Mr. McBeath was called upon to provide a box in which to bury the little body at the mouth of Grassy Coulee.

The ferry's location was moved once more during World War One, probably in 1917, when a new ferry was built and a ferryman's shack erected on the south side of the river.

The ferry broke loose from its cable several times during periods of high water in the spring and had to be rescued from downriver and brought back overland with heavy moving equipment. But it gave good service during its sixty-nine years of operation. Not many accidents have been recorded, apart from one man getting a broken jaw when helping to get the ferry out of the water.

One ferryman is remembered as running a trapline along the river in winter; another ran a little store in the ferryman's shack. George Scorgie was the ferryman for twelve years, but Fred Pugh put in the longest period on the job — twenty-seven years, according to the records.

74

DRAYTON VALLEY FERRY
(1954-57)
North Saskatchewan River   NW27-48-7-5

With two major oil discoveries in the area in 1953, the quiet little town of Drayton Valley (called Power House until 1920) became a boom town. Traffic, most of which had to go all the way to Edmonton and return along Highway 16 before the present Highway 57 was built, or cross the river on the Berrymoor ferry, suddenly became too much for the ferry to cope with, so the government put in a new ferry about three miles upriver from the present bridge and about 6½ miles from the townsite. The ferry was built at the site by Bill Katherens, the government Ferry Foreman, Bill's brother Howard, and their ferry crew. It was a standard size ferry and was operated on the cable by a motor. The road to the ferry went down the south side of the Wollschlager Coulee.

Traffic increased to the point where three ferrymen were employed in 1956, and even so, vehicles sometimes had to wait as long as three hours to get across. The cable broke twice and the ferry, which drifted on to a sandbar, had to be hauled back by caterpillar tractor. The need for a bridge to carry the heavy oilfield equipment soon became evident and the bridge on the new Highway 57 was opened to traffic in 1958, at which time the ferry was taken up to the Berrymoor Crossing for use there.

This ferry at Drumheller helped hundreds of settlers who took up land east of the river. It is seen here in 1913-14.

75

DRUMHELLER AREA FERRIES
(1902-14)
Red Deer River

Many settlers arrived in the district before the turn of the century. James Trumble and James Russell came in 1896 and both are reputed to have used some form of river crossing. Russell farmed at Nacmine and ran his cattle over the river as far as Stettler and the Hand Hills. He built a ferry opposite his home site, a large rowboat type, and transported many homesteaders going across to settle in Verdant Valley. Thomas Greentree arrived in 1902 and built and operated a ferry just east of where the present power house now stands. In the spring of 1908, two land seekers had occasion to use this craft. According to the story Mr. Greentree

> owned a row boat, a leaky one to be sure, but he told them that if one of them could row the boat while the other baled the water out of it, they could make it across the river.

Robert Allan Wigmore moved to north of Carbon in 1904 and later established a homestead on the river between Kneehill and Ghost Pine Creeks, where a well-used trail came down the hill. Wigmore built a ferry at this point to assist the many incoming settlers to get across the river, but in 1908, while he was helping to transport a load of fence posts, he was drowned. His father, Sam Wigmore, also a settler in the area, was the first ferryman on the government ferry installed "near Carbon" in 1908.

Early pioneer Ernest Horney built a ferry in Red Deer and floated it down river about 1909, carrying his wife, his large family, and all their household goods, to a point just south of the present town of Drumheller. Shortly after it was opened, in the summer of 1909, a pioneer woman recalled crossing in the ferry. "When half way over," she said, "the horses concluded that they could make better time than the ferry and only the prompt action of the men on board prevented them from plunging into the water." This ferry was taken over by Jake Leonhardt and was used to transport railroad crews and material across the river when the railroad was being built, about 1909-1910. According to the annual reports, another ferry was installed at Drumheller in 1912, although its exact location is not recorded. It was possibly for use by the crews constructing the bridge which was opened to traffic in 1914 when, the annual report states, "the Drumheller ferry was moved to Emerson's Ford."

DUNVEGAN FERRY
(1909-60)
Peace River   E½7-80-4-6

The North West Company's Fort Dunvegan, established in 1805 by

A causeway was built past the shallow waters to allow passengers to use the Dunvegan ferry in the mid-1930s. The ferry was a pontoon craft.

Archibald Macleod, was named after his ancestral home on the Isle of Skye. There is no record of any ferry being used in those early days, although it is quite likely the fort kept a boat for that purpose. The provincial government installed a ferry in 1909 to assist settlers on the old wagon road from Peace River to Grande Prairie. The famous "Bull Train," a large group of settlers from Ontario who travelled from Edmonton to Beaverlodge with eighteen teams of oxen, was the first large outfit to cross on the ferry on June 29, 1909. The ferry had broken loose on its trial run the day before, but the Bull Train had no trouble crossing. However, the hill on the south side was so steep, they had to use three teams to get one load up the hill. A. H. McQuarrie, the government engineer, was never satisfied with the state of the hill on the south side, but the water current and depth of water at the crossing (near the old Roman Catholic mission) made it the only suitable location. McQuarrie suggested blasting the south hill, but permission was not granted, so improvements had to be made to the hill and ferry approaches from time to time over the years. New cable towers were built at a new site in 1919 (near the old Hudson's Bay Co. buildings), just in case the ferry had to be moved. According to McQuarrie's later report, "sixteen years after the extra cable was installed the whole south hillside fell into the river." The ferry was moved to the new site and, about this time, Alex Holmquist, the ferryman, lost his life when the heavily loaded ferry broke loose from its cable.

77

The width of the river posed problems so the ferry was fitted with a pontoon sometime in the 1930s. Later, in the 1950s, it was propelled across the river by a tugboat.

The ferry had a long trip downriver in 1933. The *Grande Prairie Herald-Tribune* of Nov. 2, 1933, carried the following item:

> There will be no more crossing of the Peace River this fall as the ferry got caught in a flow of ice last Thursday and is now on its way to the Arctic. The ferry passed the town of Peace River at noon on the next day. Both ferrymen were aboard when it broke loose, but managed to get off in the boat which is always attached.

The craft was caught and safely snubbed on an island beyond Peace River town, and was reported to be none the worse for its thrilling thirty-mile ride.

Winter crossings were made on the ice when it was thick enough, but sometimes a "cars only" order was put into effect. In 1939 a small motor-powered scow, with a capacity for one car or truck, was put into operation for use when spring and fall ice conditions prevented the regular ferry operation.

During its fifty-one years of operation, the ferry carried thousands of people across the river. In 1953 a total of 24,500 cars were transported across during a six-month period — an average of over 2,000 per week.

Four Beaverlodge baseball players may recall the day in the summer of 1954 when they were stranded for nearly five hours on the ferry when high winds took it downriver. There was no way the players could get off and they lost their game by default!

Demands for a bridge at Dunvegan began shortly after World War Two and continued on until 1957, when work was started on a 2,000 foot long suspension bridge. This was opened to traffic in 1960, making line-ups of traffic for the ferry a thing of the past, and cutting out the 220-mile trip from Fairview to Grande Prairie in the spring and fall.

The ferry changed its classification a few times — to Class A (two ferrymen) in 1929, back to Class B (one ferryman) in 1934, and back to Class A again in 1941. In 1952 the classification appears to have changed altogether, with a captain, engineers and deckhands being officially appointed by the government. The tugboat was in operation at this time, which is probably the reason why all these operators were required.

The story of the Dunvegan ferry would not be complete without mention of ferryman "Honest Joe" Bissett who walked into the area from west of the mountains via Prince George. He operated the ferry for several years in his own way. He saw no reason why people should be in a hurry or want to cross on the ferry at night. Finally, he decided that he had had enough and took his dog and walked out of the district the way he had come in.

DURLINGVILLE FERRY
(1913-20)
North Saskatchewan   63-4/5-4

This ferry was listed on the provincial government's annual reports from 1912 to 1915 by its land location, and from 1916 to 1920 as "North of Durlingville." However, no information on this ferry has come to light.

EAST COULEE FERRY
(1930-50)
Red Deer River   28/29-27-18-4

Several petitions for a ferry at East Coulee were received by the government in 1929, and the petitioners were advised that "a ferry has been arranged." It was installed for the 1930 season and served the purpose of carrying miners over to the Atlas, Murray, Empire and other mines north of the river, as well as taking farmers and their grain to the elevators south of the river.

In 1935, district farmers wrote to the government asking them to extend daily ferry operation until midnight rather than 7:00 pm to enable them to haul all their grain. This was done for the 1935 fall period, and an extra ferryman was hired.

In 1936 the owners of the Atlas mine wrote to the government asking for permission to build and install an overhead "cage" to carry miners across the river when the ice was running, and to this the government agreed, provided Atlas would be responsible for any claim or damage arising from use of the "cage." However, in the fall of 1936 the CPR put a plank footpath across the railway bridge so that the miners could walk across.

The busy little ferry had been designated as a Class A ferry during the summer of 1936 when two ferrymen worked in shifts and a shack close to the ferry crossing was rented for the ferrymen's use.

EDMONTON FERRIES
(1882-1913)
North Saskatchewan River

Numerous references exist stating that small row boats were used to ferry Indian customers and other people across the river to trade at Fort Edmonton. However, the first commercial ferry was established

One of the busiest ferries in Alberta was the one which connected Edmonton with its neighbouring town of Strathcona. It is seen here in 1906.

by John Walter. Born in 1849 in the Orkney Islands (Scotland), Walter came to Edmonton about 1870 to build York boats for the Hudson's Bay Company. He homesteaded, and built and operated his own sawmill on what is now the area between 107 and 109 Streets and south across present Whyte Avenue. Here he built not only boats and ferries but also manufactured door frames and window sashes for early settlers.

Walter was granted a licence by the town of Edmonton in 1881 to operate a "rope" ferry, the licence giving him six miles of river, three on each side of his ferry crossing. He launched "The Belle of Edmonton" on the river in 1882, where it operated for over twenty years. A second ferry, built and installed in 1883 at the foot of today's 92nd Street to the east end of Cloverdale, was later moved to a crossing near the present Low Level Bridge, and was known as the Edmonton-Strathcona ferry, used by all travellers coming in from the south. A third ferry was built and installed by Walter at Clover Bar in 1883, and he also built ferries for other points designated by the North-West Territorial Government.

The Edmonton ferries, known as the "upper" and "lower" ferries, carried a great deal of traffic, the "lower" ferry in particular carrying most of it. By 1891, the newly-formed Edmonton Cartage Co. was hauling so much freight of all kinds, plus the mail and the daily bus service between Edmonton and Strathcona, that it formed the

Edmonton Ferry Company and installed a free ferry about 100 yards from the "lower" crossing to carry all the freight of the cartage company.

In 1893, William Humberstone, who had operated the "lower" ferry for several years, also had ideas about running his own free ferry, but his lawyers advised him that he could only do this by buying land on each side of the river for ferry landings, and forming a kind of club or partnership, the members of which could use the ferry free of charge. Apparently this did not materialize, but in 1893 Humberstone was granted a licence by the town of Edmonton to "establish and run two ferries on the River Saskatchewan between the south and northwesterly banks," and in 1894 Humberstone's tender of $500, payable to the Town of Edmonton for the running of both ferries, was accepted over Walters' tender of $10. This apparently was for the two Humberstone ferries at the "lower" crossing, as further tenders were sought for the operation of the "upper" ferry.

In May of 1894, some controversy arose regarding the tolls charged on the lower ferries, and later that year, in November, Humberstone accused the Edmonton Ferry Company, operated by James Dinner, owner of the Edmonton Cartage Company, of unlawfully running their free ferry, thereby infringing on Humberstone's rights as the operator of the licensed ferry for which he now had to pay the town of Edmonton $600 per year.

The case went to the supreme court, where Judge C. B. Rouleau eventually ruled, in February 1895, that both lower ferries should operate as toll ferries, and that the Town of Edmonton had no right to grant a licence for the exclusive right of a ferry as they had to Humberstone. Humberstone then withdrew his case against Dinner and decided to take action against the town, which had sold him something it had no right to sell. At this time the Town of Edmonton established toll rates to be charged by all three ferries, and Walter, Humberstone and Dinner were requested to apply for licences under these tariffs —five cents for a single horse and rig, or a horse and rider, and ten cents for a double team.

All three ferries, two at the lower crossing and Walter's ferry at the upper crossing, apparently continued to operate satisfactorily and in harmony until the Low Level bridge was opened to traffic in 1900. The Walter ferry continued to operate until 1913, being the only method of crossing in that area until the High Level bridge was built.

Winter crossings at Edmonton were made on the ice, but during the few weeks in the spring and fall when ice conditions made crossings impossible, freight teams, mail and supplies piled up on each side of

Travel on the Edson-Grande Prairie Trail would have been virtually impossible without the essential ferry crossings. Above is the ferry on Little Smoky River, in the Pass Creek area, in the 1911-14 period.

Ferrymen sometimes had more than their share of problems. Here a team of horses decide to make an early departure from the ferry on Little Smoky River near Pass Creek about 1911-14.

82

the river waiting to be ferried across. Later, a "cage" was installed on the cable so that urgent supplies and mail could be moved, presumably at the lower crossing, although this is not confirmed.

There are many stories of the Edmonton ferries. One time a group of men on an all-night "spree" stole the ferry and tried to cross the river, only to be stranded in midstream. Another time a lumberjack ran for a ferry which was just pulling away from shore. The ferry didn't wait and neither did the lumberjack — he jumped into the river and raced the ferry across the river. One early settler who came overland by wagon from Winnipeg brought all his household goods with him, including a small rosewood piano. As the ferry had stopped running for the night, the family camped on the river bank and they played the old familiar tunes on the little piano, joining in song, with their voices floating along the river valley in the cool night air. The following morning, with the piano wrapped in the heavy quilts and blankets which protected it on its journey, they loaded everything on to the ferry. Just as they reached the opposite side of the river, the piano fell off into the shallow water, but it was rescued and suffered no real damage. It probably was one of the first pianos to cross the North Saskatchewan river on a ferry.

EDSON-GRANDE PRAIRIE TRAIL FERRIES
(1911-1949)

Four ferries were built and installed by the provincial government in 1911 to assist the hundreds of early settlers travelling the Edson-Grande Prairie Trail. This "short cut" to the north was just a narrow path cut through the tall, dark forest. The muskeg, deep mud and steep hills saw hundreds of early settlers struggling along, hauling themselves and their belongings, almost eaten alive by mosquitos and black flies, unloading and reloading many times when they got stuck in the mud. The government's engineer, A. H. McQuarrie surveyed parts of the trail already marked out by a group of Grande Prairie residents in 1910, and he and his crews started to improve it by corduroying the worst parts and building ferries to cross the wider rivers. They set up a ferry camp close to the Athabasca River crossing at Mile 53 to build three of the ferries.

After crossing the Athabasca benchland, travellers slipped and slid down "Breakneck Hill" to the river where they were thankful to reach Severson's stopping place and, according to one traveller, they "found there a couple who had a nice garden . . . and they ran a ferry across the river . . ." On again over the trail they continued to the Baptiste (now Berland) River, where old John Anderson, the ferryman, lived in

Charlie Magnusson is seen here with the first Elk Point ferry in 1914.

a tent during the summer months. The next major river on the trail was the Little Smoky where, in the Pass Creek area, the third ferry was waiting to transport them. The first travellers in 1911 arrived there to find that "the ferry was not finished." They had to wait there for about ten days "until some men arrived with the cable," before they could cross. Further along the trail the Tony and House rivers were apparently shallow enough to ford before the long haul north to Sturgeon Lake, where they could rest for a while before making their way west to cross the Big Smoky River at the fourth ferry, their 250-mile journey to Grand Prairie almost ended.

These ferries on the Edson-Grande Prairie Trail were kept busy during the summer months, and the ferrymen surely earned their wages in helping the settlers to load and unload all their worldly goods.

By 1918, according to the annual report, "traffic on the Trail was so light that the [first] three ferries were maintained by the province for travellers to operate themselves." The fourth ferry on the trail, re-named Goodwin's Crossing, remained in operation until 1949 (see Goodwin's Crossing Ferry).

ELDORENA FERRY
(1908-67)
North Saskatchewan River   NE23-57-20-4

The 1908 annual report notes that "the old Victoria ferry was moved] to a point north of Lamont on the North Saskatchewan River" which was the post office settlement of Eldorena. This developed into a small village in a mixed farming and stock raising district settled by Ukrainian pioneers.

The ferry enabled farmers east of the river to cross to the railway, and although it remained in service for almost sixty years, its existence was apparently uneventful.

ELK POINT FERRY
(1913-50)
North Saskatchewan River   SE25-56-7-4

Charlie Hood had a general store at Elk Point and also operated a scow across the river to assist settlers coming into the area after 1909. Although the name Elk Point was established in 1909, the crossing, in the vicinity of the old fur trading posts of Buckingham House and Fort George, was known locally as "Hood's Crossing" for many years.

The government built a ferry for this crossing in 1913 and floated it downriver from Edmonton, but as there were no accompanying barges to guide it, it floated right past the crossing and was used elsewhere. As a result another ferry had to be built for Elk Point. As the area developed and more settlers arrived, it became a very busy crossing. Stock days saw waiting line-ups over a mile long, with animals squealing and bellowing their protests on their way to the stockyards north of the river. In the evenings, wagons lined up to return on the ferry, laden with goods and supplies purchased with the stock cheques. Every fall, too, there was a desperate rush to get the harvested grain across on the hardworking little ferry to the elevators before the river ice started to form.

Some time in the 1930s, ferryman Alf Monkman and Dr. F. G. Miller, the local doctor, rigged up a platform known as the "Jigger," to be used in emergencies during spring and fall when the ferry could not be used. If Dr. Miller had to cross the river on an emergency call, he and Alf would crouch low on the "jigger" as it sped down the cable to the middle of the river, then stand up and haul themselves up the other half of the cable. While the doctor visited his patient, Alf would build a fire and await the doctor's return, both repeating the crossing in the same way. Sometimes the doctor would be called out again the same night, and he and Alf would do the same thing all over again!

The government built and installed a larger "cage" for emergency crossings about 1935 — a much safer way of crossing, known locally as the "go-devil." This was used to transport mail and supplies and could also be used by passengers. About 1939, the "go-devil" loaded with a group of local boys fell about twenty feet on to the river ice, but fortunately none of the passengers was hurt.

EMERSON'S FORD FERRY
(1914-18)
Red Deer River   33-22-14-4

According to the government's annual reports, the ferry from Drumheller was moved to Emerson's Ford in 1914, near John Emerson's ranch buildings. A bridge was built in 1918, but it was washed out in 1929, rebuilt, and washed away again in 1947. A bridge was built in 1960, on Highway 36, not far from Emerson's Ford.

EMPRESS-WEST FERRY
(1913-18)
Red Deer River   22/23-23-1-4

Early crossings at this point were made by rowboat — sometimes two rowboats "planked" together and poled across. The "Englebrecht" ferry, according to local history, was used before the government ferry was installed. It carried supplies across the river near Bill Highmoor's place and was apparently operated by local rancher, William Englebrecht. Local history also recalls a "Black Bill" as the ferryman. The ferry was a small one, about ten feet wide and the length of a wagon, with a cable made out of five strands of twisted barbed wire. "Black Bill" is reputed to have charged $2.00 for crossings on his little ferry — a stiff toll in those early days.

In 1912, the Hurlburt brothers and Martin Carmangay are said to have taken farmers across the river in their small boats free of charge in protest against the exorbitant rates charged by "Black Bill."

The government built and installed an official ferry in 1913, known as the west ferry. It ceased to operate in 1918 although the cable towers remained for many years to mark the old ferry crossing.

EMPRESS-EAST FERRY
(1916-22)
Red Deer River   On 4th Meridian

Known locally as the "Dargie" ferry, this crossing was on property owned by early settler John Dargie who arrived in the district about 1897 with W. T. "Red Deer" Smith of Big Barn fame. Dargie, a popular man, had a house by the river but it is not known whether he ever acted as the ferryman. Allie Fjeldberg did run the ferry at one period, however, date unknown. Before the ferry was installed so history recalls, Dargie used to cross the river with his clothes carried on top of his head and dress himself on the other side; also, living so close to the river, "he trained his chickens to swim."

EMPRESS-SOUTH FERRY
(1924-61)
South Saskatchewan River

According to annual reports, this ferry was installed in 1924, and continued in operation for about thirty-eight years, until the Sandy Point bridge was built. In 1929, it was designated as a Class A ferry, with two ferrymen, so was obviously a busy crossing.

The 1940 annual report lists a "proposed ferry at Empress" but there is no further reference to this or any indication as to whether one was supplied.

ENTWISTLE FERRY
(1909-22)
Pembina River   33/34-53-7-5

The government installed this ferry in 1909 as "West of Wabamun." The 1910 annual report indicates that "the ferry over the Pembina River west of Wabamun was moved to a point over the Pembina at "Hood's Crossing." However, the 1911 report still showed a ferry west of Wabamun. The 1912-13 reports list a ferry at Entwistle, and the 1914 report indicates that "the ferry on the Pembina River moved from Entwistle to Matthews Crossing."

Annual reports 1915 to 1922 show a ferry still at Entwistle, although a bridge was built there in 1910. Inquiries have failed to turn up any information about the "West of Wabamun" and "Entwistle" ferries. Hood's Crossing was probably the Sunniebend crossing where ferry service started in 1910; a Charles Hood lived in that area.

EUNICE FERRY
(1915-25)
Pembina River   SE13-62-1-5

Wilfred Budgen, one of the first settlers in the district, remembered this ferry, but had no information about it. It was listed on the annual reports from 1915 to 1923 as "Eunice," and as "Dapp" in 1924 and 1925.

EYREMORE FERRY
(1911-20)
Bow River   13-17-17-4

Oldtimers recall that "the first ferry was straight west of Rainier," running across the river between land owned by the Eyres and Moore families, hence the name Eyremore. This was probably a private ferry, owned and operated by W. H. "Daddy" Moore before 1911, when the government installed its own ferry at the above location. This was also listed in the annual reports as the Eyremore ferry until 1920, when a bridge was built at the crossing. Local history gives the name of John Erickson as the ferryman. He lived near the crossing, but it is not known whether he operated the ferry for the entire ten years it was in operation.

Jerome Durand, interviewed at Carstairs in 1983, recalled a day in 1914 when, as a young lad, he helped his father to deliver a herd of cattle north of the river. When they got to the river, it was full of running ice and many rigs were lined up on the riverbank waiting for the ferry to start running. It was not until 7:00 in the evening that the ice started to thin out a little so that they could cross. They had to work all night, until early next morning, poling the ferry back and forth across the river to get all the rigs and cattle across. Finally, on the return trip to the ferryman's home side, the ferry got stuck in the ice and everyone had to start all over again to dig it out so that ferryman Erickson could get home.

There was also a private ferry, date unknown, owned and operated by a couple of local men, McCoubrey and Koepke, who used it for hauling coal across the river just west of the island. As there were no proper approaches, foot passengers and vehicles could not use it.

FALHER FERRY
(1944-63)
Little Smoky River   NW25-75-22-5

There is no information recorded about this ferry, apart from the annual reports which list it as "South of Falher"; its location was between White Mud Creek and present day Guy. It is assumed that it was installed to carry employees and equipment of the White Mud oilfields. In 1959, the ferry from the Grovedale Crossing on the Wapiti River was moved to the South of Falher crossing.

FAWCETT-SOUTH FERRY
(1921-51)
Pembina River   3/4-64-1-5

The district to the south and west of the hamlet of Fawcett (formerly French Creek) was mainly swamp land which caused two separate districts, the Ferry School District and the Chain School District, and two ferries were necessary as the swamp could not be crossed.

The south ferry was installed in response to many requests from war veterans who had taken up farming east of the river, and wanted to get across to the railway and the store. Ferry service was irregular

This Fawcett ferry was located in a sylvan glade of picturesque beauty. It was a pleasant place to be as long as it wasn't raining.

for a few years — in 1924 a ferryman operated only two days a week, days when the train came through Fawcett. At other times, the ferry was used by the public themselves which was not always satisfactory, as many times a settler would take the ferry across to the east bank early in the morning and it would remain there all day, causing a day's delay for others wishing to cross from the west. A regular ferryman who ran the ferry on a daily basis was appointed in 1926, and a new ferry and ferryman's house was built in 1928.

The ferry approaches were not reinforced with gravel, but consisted only of earth which turned into thick mud in wet weather, making it difficult for vehicles to get on or off the ferry.

Elwood Boyd of Fawcett helped to rebuild the cable towers in 1930; he recalls a man who drove onto the ferry one night in a 1929 Model A car without waiting for the ferryman's signal to embark. The restraining cable was not in place and he drove off the opposite end of the ferry into about eight feet of water. He managed to get out of his car and stand on its roof until rescued by the ferryman, the car being hauled out by tractor.

FAWCETT-WEST FERRY
(1928-51)
NW18-64-1-5

The west ferry was only five miles from the south ferry by road, but about fifteen miles by river, and it provided a quicker means of crossing to Fawcett for people north-west of the hamlet. Even after a bridge was built near the south ferry, the swamp prevented some people from using it and they had to travel down to the Jarvie bridge to get back up to Fawcett.

Both the south and west ferries were gathering places on summer weekends for residents to socialize at picnics and swimming parties. Joe Dawkins, ferryman at the west ferry for eighteen years, was well-liked by everyone and welcomed visitors.

Oldtimers recall many Sundays in the 1930s when large groups of people would spend the day with Joe at the ferry, with an eight-gallon keg of beer, and cheese and crackers. One such Sunday, Joe was poling the ferry across when the pole slipped and Joe fell into the river while the ferry continued on its way. Joe was about sixty-five years old at the time, but swam across after the ferry.

Both the west and south ferry crossings are now overgrown with trees and brush, and the approaches filled in with silt, but memories remain.

FINNEGAN FERRY
(1913-present)
Red Deer River   SE18-25-15-4

The location of this ferry was at a ford which had previously been used by many early travellers and settlers. To gauge the depth of the river, if travellers could see the top of a white rock in the river, it was safe for them to ford.

John Finnegan, who came from Scotland to Gleichen in the 1880s, took up homestead land in the district in 1903. He and his wife (reputed to be the best pastrycook in the West) kept a stopping house and also operated the ferry after it was installed in 1913. The ferry and the district were both named for John Finnegan.

There has been a ferry at the Finnegan Crossing for over seventy years and it has apparently led a quite uneventful existence as not much of its history has been recorded. One story is told, however, of the police trying to catch some local "moonshiners" during prohibition days. They rode back and forth on the ferry for two days, waiting for the moonshiners to show up before returning to Bassano after their unfruitful surveillance. As soon as they were out of sight, the ferryman lifted the trapdoor in the ferry deck and took out two kegs of the illicit liquor — the police had been riding on top of them for two days!

The ferry today still carries passengers and cars, including hunters travelling to hunting grounds east of the Wintering Hills.

90

FLATBUSH FERRY
(1931-57)
Pembina River   SW35-65-2-5

This ferry apparently had an uneventful, unrecorded life of sixteen years. It was installed to transport settlers across the river to the railway.

FORBESVILLE FERRY
(1917-60)
North Saskatchewan River   5/8-54-1-4

The Forbes family, early pioneers in the area, gave the district and the ferry its name, by which it was unofficially known for forty-four years. Although the Forbesville ferry was only a few miles from the Meridian ferry to the east and the Lea Park ferry to the west, it obviously had sufficient traffic to enable it to remain in operation for so long. The Indian Reserve No. 120 was immediately north-west of the ferry, adding to the flow of travellers to the south. The village of South Ferriby was just west of the ferry, by which name the ferry was sometimes known locally.

Bobby Roberton, ferryman for 15 years from 1929 to 1944, was well-known and well-liked locally, and is remembered as a most agreeable, kind and humorous man. Another ferryman in the early 1920s, Bill McCusker, decided to cross the river one spring while the ice was running. He and a friend sat astride a plank attached to the ferry cable, but as the cable sagged badly in the middle they hit the icy water midstream and had to be rescued. The only comment McCusker made when he reached dry land was that he had lost all his tobacco in the river!

The Forbesville ferry was plagued over the years by the many sandbars which built up in the river and as these had to be dredged away from time to time, the ferry became difficult and costly to operate. Finally, in 1960, traffic having been considerably reduced since the Lea Park bridge was built in 1957, the Forbesville ferry was discontinued.

FORT KIPP FERRY
(c. 1874-99)
Oldman River

Although there is no record of a ferry in use when Fort Kipp was originally built in 1870 when it was used as a whisky trading post, it seems likely that some kind of craft would have been used to transport people and supplies across the river. However, when the whisky traders were routed and the North-West Mounted Police took over

Fort Kipp in 1874, they apparently operated their own ferry at this location. This was the scene of a tragedy in 1882 when Nicholas Sheran was drowned while escorting members of the police.

In 1886, William Long and Richard Urch built a ranch, a stopping house and a post office at the site; they also operated a ferry which was built at Fort Macleod and floated downriver to Kipp. Tolls on this ferry seem to have varied according to the load to be carried. The Lethbridge to Fort Macleod stagecoach got across for only $1.00 but a bull team or a twelve-horse rig was charged $3.00 or $3.50, quite a large sum for ferriage in those days. A member of the police, on horseback, paid only 25 cents whereas other travellers were charged 50 cents. On one trip the ferry carried eight teams of oxen and three wagons loaded with coal; and in May, 1891, a large beef herd was ferried across, a long and difficult task.

> . . . On 27 May, 1887, owing to the very high water in the Old Man's River, an accident occurred at Kipp which caused the death of two horses of 'D' Division, and very nearly caused the deaths of four others and three constables. The disaster occurred owing to the breaking of a wheel of the ferryboat. (NWMP Annual Report, 1887)
>
> There is also a private ferry over the Old Man's River at Kipp, provided by the enterprise of the keeper of the stopping house there. He declines, however, to accept licensed ferry fares on the ground that the rates would not pay him . . . This is the spot at which a poor freighter had his string team swept away last spring . . . 15 of his horses were lost. (NWMP Annual Report 1889)
>
> There are two ferries in this district, one at Kipp, one at Macleod . . . but they are seldom run when most needed for fear of accidents. (NWMP Annual Report 1890)

These reports of the North West Mounted Police indicate the difficulties of ferry crossings at Kipp; the river at this spot could be extremely fast and dangerous after heavy rains. Traffic on the ferry decreased when the railroad between Lethbridge and Fort Macleod took over from the stagecoach and bull teams. When bridges were built at Lethbridge and Fort Macleod, the ferry was discontinued.

FORT MACLEOD FERRY
(1883-92 & 1902)
Oldman River

The North-West Mounted Police built their fort in 1874 and Police Surgeon R. B. Nevitt, who spent the first winter there, mentioned a small bridge in his diary, which, it is assumed, was used to cross the ever-changing river. However, police records indicate that in 1879 they "paid William Gladstone $75.00 for a ferryboat for the Belly River" and they also paid Richard Kennefick $19.20 for "repairing a ferry boat." This may have been the ferry at Fort Kipp, which was on the Belly River.

In 1880 the river changed course completely, running south of the fort, which had been built on Gallagher's Island, instead of north, causing all communication to be cut off for a short time. The police report for that year indicated that the Indians across the river "were starving as no food could be got to them until a ferry was constructed." However, the report goes on to say that "a bridge was constructed" as soon as the river settled in its new bed.

In 1883, E. T. Galt's NorthWest Coal & Navigation Company built a sawmill at Ford Macleod, and Galt applied to the North-West Territorial Government for a ferry licence, apparently for a crossing on the river north-east of the fort. This did away with the dangerous crossing known as "Death Ford" where many lives had been lost. Galt received a letter from Lieutenant-Governor E. Dewdney in Winnipeg, dated 18 May 1883:

> I am in receipt of your application for a Ferry Licence for a ferry on the Old Mans River at or near Fort Macleod . . . the charter will date from 1st July 1883, by which time it is expected the Ferry will be complete and in a position to be inspected by our Inspector.

The Rev. Dr. John McLean in his *Memories of Macleod,* recalled that "there was a bathing pond and a ferry boat on the main street," in the 1880s.

After the river had changed its course in 1880, it became imperative that the fort should be moved, but it was not until May 1884 that the police moved into their new barracks south of the river.

The ferry apparently continued to operate after a fashion until a bridge was built in 1892. The police mentioned the ferry several times in their annual reports, mostly pointing out its inefficiency. According to their 1888 report the ferry did not run at all that year.

> . . . no ferries operating in the Macleod district . . . the people positively declining to run them as the rate allowed for tolls and the rates charged are exorbitant and the traveller is at the mercy of the owner of the ferry who can, and does, cross him when he is ready and at his own price.
>
> . . . frequently, when the ferry is most required, the violence of the stream prohibits its use . . . in the spring it is impossible to get out of Macleod to the north . . . without risking life and outfit during high water . . . loss of life is constantly occurring in consequence.

The 1890 annual report stated:

> there are two ferries . . . one at Kipp and one at Macleod . . . but they are seldom run when most needed, for fear of accidents.

The bridge built in 1892 was washed away in high water in 1902, when a ferry was again put into operation at Macleod until a stronger bridge was opened to traffic in 1903. The ferry was then floated up river to the Pincher Creek crossing.

In 1909 the provincial Department of Public Works paid the sum of $85.62 for material and labour for the "Old Man River Ferry, near Macleod," but this ferry is not shown on any other lists or reports.

FORT SASKATCHEWAN FERRIES
(1875-1905)
North Saskatchewan River

When the North-West Mounted Police settled into their barracks at Fort Saskatchewan on the south bank of the river in 1875, the little settlement of Lamoureaux on the north bank was already flourishing. Joseph and Francois Lamoureaux had arrived at the spot in 1872 and had built their little community of log cabins. Joseph had brought his family from Quebec; they were homesteading by 1874, and in 1875 they were operating a small rowboat ferry across the river to the new fort. This ferry was used by the police and local settlers in the area until 1880, when a cable ferry was installed under licence of the North-West Territorial Government. This served river crossing traffic until 1886, when the cable broke and the ferry was carried off downriver. It was hauled back and put into service again, but in 1887 a drifting scow from Edmonton, torn from its mooring, wrecked the ferry and cable so severely that new ones had to be built and installed. This ferry operated until 1894 when it sank with a load of bricks and lumber and about a dozen head of horses. The next ferry was put into service in 1895 and two years later, the NWMP reported its problems, stating that the ferry

> . . . was purchased by the North-West Territorial Government . . . from Mr. Joseph Lamoureaux and is now run under the management of a committee taken from some of the prominent businessmen in the village, and the crossings are now much cheaper than in former years.
>
> During the month of June, owing to unprecedented rains, the river rose to an abnormal height, carrying away the ferry cable and the ferry itself was carried downriver a considerable distance before it was recovered. This state of affairs caused a considerable amount of inconvenience to settlers on both sides of the river . . .

The Annual Report of the North-West Mounted Police for 1900-01 stated:

> The ferry at Fort Saskatchewan is operated by the village authorities without the payment of any bonus as the fees from the large amount of ferriage at that point pay for the operation of the ferry."

94

It was carried downriver again in 1902 but was hauled back and resumed service. Settlement of the area on both sides of the river continued and the ferry shuttled back and forth carrying all manner of cargoes. During the periods when the ferry was unable to operate crossings had to be made on the ice or at times when the river was low enough to be forded.

Nora Omness Ronaghan Williamson recalled a story told to her by her parents of their crossing on this ferry in 1899. After their hair-raising crossing on the Edmonton-Strathcona ferry, they arrived at the top of the hill leading to the Fort Saskatchewan ferry on their way to their homestead. Mr. Omness had to stand on the doubletrees as they drove down the steep hill and the horses, crowding one another as they came to a stop on the ferry, had to be calmed by members of the Omness family. The cable wheels began to squeal as the loaded ferry left the shore and the family's dog, who refused to get on the ferry, swam across after them among all the debris, driftwood, and trees, which was coming downriver. They got across safely but were glad that their ferry crossings were over, at least for a while.

FORT VERMILION FERRY
(1916-74)
Peace River   SW28-108-13-5

Settlement of the Fort Vermilion area began as early as 1836, and by 1897 the North-West Mounted Police reported a population of 168 people.

In 1908 an agricultural sub-station was built there by the federal government, and in 1909 a petition, written in French, was received by the provincial government asking for a ferry at the settlement. However, a survey showed that the river was too wide for a cable ferry and the river banks too steep for approaches to be made. A steam ferry was suggested, also a small steamer which belonged to the Hudson's Bay Company in Edmonton, but both suggestions were rejected, and it was not until 1916 that a ferry was at last provided. In his memoirs, A. H. McQuarrie recalled:

> . . . my memory is somewhat hazy as to what two scows were floated to Fort Vermilion where they were installed near the trading posts under the direction of George Mills. There is an island at that point so a ferry was installed on each channel, with one man to operate both. As the island was covered with brush he was not always able to see approaching traffic, which was very light in those days . . . . . I later examined the river . . . the only suitable location was about two miles further upstream . . . some residents wanted the ferry to remain where it was, some wanted it moved. It caused quite a furore. When the Peace River bridge was built, the power ferry from that crossing was moved down and put into service at Fort Vermilion.

This power ferry, operated by a large motor, served travellers for years, but not always satisfactorily. One time the motor boke down and a little "kicker" motor was put in as a stopgap. However, this was too small and it, too, broke up and fell apart one day when the ferry was in midstream. On this occasion the ferry and passengers were rescued by the parish priest who went out with the parish motor boat.

A new ferry was built and installed in 1934, after the old one had been wrecked when the flooding river almost devastated the whole settlement of Fort Vermilion. New cable and towers also had to be provided, but the ferry was still motor-powered. There was no spare motor and parts were unobtainable locally, so very often when the motor broke down, the ferry was stranded, sometimes for days and weeks at a time. At times like this, as well as in the spring and fall, the settlement was completely isolated, and supplies and mail had to be taken in by freight plane. In the winter an ice bridge was made on which wagons, cars, trucks, animals and pedestrians crossed.

Canadian Coachways buses, too, used the ferry, and in the winters, if the ice bridge was not strong enough, passengers had to be unloaded on the south bank of the river. One lady cab driver made her passengers get out and walk across the ice while she drove the cab across the creaking ice bridge with the doors open in case she had to jump out.

A brand new ferry was put into service in 1962, with no cable or motor, but propelled by a "pusher" tug with a 120 hp diesel engine. This pushed the ferry back and forth across the river until 1974, when the new bridge was opened to traffic by Lt. Gov. Ralph Steinhauer. This was a great day and the beginning of a new era for Fort Vermilion, no longer isolated from the south. To the ferryman and other residents, the ferry had been a way of life for so many years — they no doubt felt a little sad on their last ride on the old ferry.

GARRINGTON FERRY
(1908-62)
Red Deer River   27-34-4-5

The first ferry at this point was installed in 1908 and described as being "West of Olds" at 27-34-4-W5, which was where the present Highway 587 crosses the river. This apparently was the old Niddrie's Crossing (Derbytown) site. In spite of the fact that the river here had been surveyed in 1907 and pronounced unsuitable for either a ferry or a bridge, a ferry was installed in response to petitions and letters from local residents. However, it was not a satisfactory site and petitioners asking for a bridge at McDougall's Crossing (Sundre) complained to the government that "at times we are cut off from medical aid, groceries and mail for two months at a time." William Niddrie, the nearest settler to the river, wrote to the Minister of Public Works that:

> . . . there are wagons and livery rigs at my place every day trying to get across the river and very often they have to go back to Olds. I pulled a settler and his team out of the river last week . . . if I had been five minutes later they would have drowned . . . there was a sad accident in the river last night. We got out the settlers, who were just alive, but their team and wagon went down the river.

These pleas apparently resulted in bridges being built at both locations, Sundre and Niddrie's Crossing, in 1908, when the ferry was moved downriver to a spot near Garrington.

This part of the Red Deer River was extremely changeable and treacherous. Each spring the flood waters altered the main channel, creating sand and gravel bars, and making it impossible to operate the ferry. It had to be moved several times for this reason over the years, and each time the municipal district had to prepare new approach roads.

The bridge at Niddrie's Crossing was washed away in the floods of 1915-16, and a ferry was installed at the crossing in 1917 to replace it. This remained in operation until 1925. The Garrington ferry, according to the annual reports, was abandoned in 1916 and does not re-appear on the reports again until 1925 when the Niddrie ferry was discontinued.

The Garrington ferry had to contend with the strong current of the Red Deer River. Note the current board at the side of the ferry, used to deflect the force of the stream.

The Garrington ferry remained in operation until 1962, operating during the summer months each years, except for 1925-26, when it operated throughout the winter months. Winter crossings were made on the ice, and in spring and fall travellers had to go round by the Sundre bridge.

Mrs. Gladys Smith of Olds recalled a spring day about 1954 when she and her husband reached the ferry just as a herd of cattle were about to cross. The river was too high for them to ford so the owner had decided to take them across on the ferry. A pile of hay on the ferry dock coaxed the first load of cattle on and they were ferried across. Then the trouble started! Some of the cows and their calves got separated and the cows were in full voice calling to their offspring, some of whom had already crossed. As the ferry started off with its second load. some of the calves panicked and jumped into the river and Mr. and Mrs. Smith watched in horror as some of them disappeared underneath the moving ferry. However, they all came out on the other side and were swept down river, eventually being lassoed and brought to safety.

There were many ferrymen at Garrington, but mention should be made of Ernie Meissner, who ran it for almost thirty years. He was assisted by an extra ferryman for the last twenty years until the Garrington bridge was completed in 1962.

GENESEE FERRY
(1906, 1917-66)
North Saskatchewan River   E16-51-3-5

This area on the bend of the river saw many travellers prior to settlement; an old trail to Lac. Ste. Anne ran north of the river and crossed at a ford.

In 1906, with settlers arriving and with several sawmills and much logging activity in the area, a better means of river crossing for teams and loaded wagons was necessary. Local timber man, Charlie Cropley, built a scow large enough to carry such loads. This craft, which was rowed or poled across by several men, served its purpose for several years. Then in 1910 Cropley built a cable ferry with permission from the Alberta government, providing that it would also be used to serve the general public. Travellers, at one time, used to light a fire on the river bank and when he saw the smoke, Cropley would go down to the ferry to take them across. About the same time, the Scheideman family, about four miles north-east of the Cropley, built and operated their own ferry near their homestead.

These two ferries provided the river crossings until 1917, when the government built and installed its own ferry. Until 1923 this was listed

A settler had a full load of supplies for his crossing of the Big Smoky River on Goodwin's ferry. This view was in 1912.

in the annual reports as "Fraser(s) Landing" as it was close to where D. R. Fraser had his sawmill. From 1924 onwards, it was listed as Genesee, the name under which the post office had been incorporated in 1916.

The Cropley ferry broke away from its cable in 1913 and again in the extremely high water of 1915 when it drifted away altogether and was seen passing through Edmonton about six hours later. The government ferry also fell victim many times to the river hazards. In 1928, rising water and floating driftwood left it sitting several feet out of the water on top of a pile of snagged driftwood; the same thing happened in 1944. In 1946 an ice jam caused so much strain on the cable that it had to be cut with a welding torch to avoid having the cable towers pulled over. In 1947 the ferry turned broadside in midstream, breaking the anchor bolt on the cable, and it floated off several hundred feet downriver with three passengers on board.

A motor was installed on the ferry in 1955. This kept it going until the fall of 1966 whe the Genesee bridge was opened to traffic.

GOODWIN CROSSING FERRY
(1911-49)
Big Smoky River   NE17-72-2-6

In 1910 the Goodwin brothers ran a stopping place on the flats east of the river where there was an old ford which had been used by the

Indians and early fur traders. They also had a boat in which they took travellers across the river for ten cents a trip. In the same year, the last part of the Edson-Grande Prairie Trail was blazed from Sturgeon Lake and as soon as this was completed the government installed a ferry which was first listed as being on the "Edson-Grande Prairie Road." From 1912 to 1915 it was shown in the annual reports as "Edson Trail," in 1916 as "Bezansons," and from 1917 to 1920 as "Nr. Mouth of Wapiti River." In 1921, both "Mouth of Wapiti River" and "Bezansons" were listed, in 1922 "Bezansons" only, and in 1923 the name changed to "Goodwins Crossing," by which name it was listed through to 1949.

The ferry carried a large amount of traffic from 1911 to 1918 as the fourth ferry on the Trail. In 1913 the cable broke and the ferry was carried about eighteen miles downriver with the mail stage still on deck. This loss of the ferry caused considerable delay to travellers until a new ferry was built and installed about a month later.

Apparently anticipating the extension of the Canadian Northern Railway several miles upriver from Goodwin Crossing, pioneer promoter and writer, A. M. Bezanson, established his new townsite in 1914 on the west bank of the river just north of the mouth of the Wapiti River. In the winter of 1914 residents of this new little settlement asked for and received a ferry. This was swept downriver in 1915 and the old ferry from Goodwins was taken up as a replacement. The river was surveyed in 1921 and as a sandbar was forming which would make it difficult for the ferry to cross, it was moved back to Goodwins, but still listed as "Bezansons."

In the meantime, William Moody and his family settled in their homestead on the west bank of the river near Goodwins. There they ran a stopping house for many years and also operated the ferry, which became known locally as "Moody's Crossing."

After its years of service on the Edson-Grande Prairie Trail, the Goodwin ferry continued its busy life. As early as 1933, traffic was so great that a bridge "was an absolute necessity." In 1933 also, much speculation arose by the discovery of the foreleg of a moose embedded in the cable "deadman" east of the river. The theory was that the moose had been caught by the front leg between two young trees at some time and died, leaving the leg bone in the wood.

In the 1940s, the crossing was used extensively by traffic to the north, including vehicles on the Alaska Highway. The ferry approaches were widened in 1947 and a larger ferry was built to accommodate the trucks, house trailers, and heavy freighters coming through from the United States. First waiting to cross on the ferry after it was launched for the 1948 season were four taxi cabs from San Francisco en route to Anchorage, Alaska. They had waited two days for the ice to clear and when the crossing was finally possible, traffic was lined up on both sides of the river for about a mile. Some travellers had been waiting for days and as there was not enough accommodation at the crossing, people were sleeping in their cars, some with blankets loaned by the ferryman. The only small restaurant supplied meals, but even so, food was becoming scarce as the ferry launching was delayed by the river ice.

There was much heavy traffic all that year, sometimes 157 vehicles a day, with as many as forty to fifty large heavy vehicles lined up on both sides of the river. The little ferry could only take one at a time — in fact, one large vehicle had to be taken apart to be carried across. This increased traffic was caused primarily by a longshoreman's strike in Vancouver. This was added to the traffic of lumber trucks from DeBolt and Crooked Creek en route to the mills in Grande Prairie. Instead of being hauled out of the river at the first sign of ice in the fall of that year, the ferry continued to operate with a steam boiler melting the ice underneath it until an ice bridge could be formed a little further upriver.

The pressure of traffic resulted in materials and machinery for a bridge appearing at the site before the end of the year, and by the fall of 1949, William Moody, then 84 years old, stood on the deck of a new steel five-span bridge, with 12,000 other people who had gathered for the bridge opening.

GRASSY LAKE FERRY
(1910-25)
Oldman River

The following information is taken from the annual reports of the Alberta Department of Public Works:

1906-1909	— Ferry on the Belly River at Taber
1910	— Ferry moved to N. of Purple Springs (11/14-15-4)
1910-1913	— Ferry North of Coaldale (Nolan's)
1914	— Ferry moved to Grand Forks (Grassy Lake)
1915-1925	— Ferries at Purple Springs and Grassy Lake (Grand Forks) operated by the public at their own convenience.

Although there had been a few settlers in this area since 1893, these had been mostly railway employees, section men and the like, the villages of Purple Springs and Grassy Lake being merely "whistle stops." After the turn of the century when the area was filling with homesteaders and land north of the river was being settled, it became necessary for farmers to get their grain and supplies across the river to the railhead. As a result, a ferry was installed in 1906 north of Taber, but when a bridge was finally completed there in 1910, after being washed away in 1908, this ferry was floated down river to a point "N. of Purple Springs."

When the Coaldale ferry was moved in 1914, it was located on the Furman ranch near Grand Forks.

Both ferries were listed in the annual reports by the names of "Purple Springs" and "Grassy Lake" at least until 1922, and were maintained without ferrymen by the province so that people had to operate them at their own convenience. "Convenience" however, was not always applicable as both ferries were often to be found at the opposite side of the river from the would-be user. Rowboats were supplied to enable a person to cross and bring the ferry back to where his grain, livestock or supplies were waiting. Many times, however, both rowboats and ferries were anchored on the wrong side of the river.

At Grassy Lake, the Furman Ranch cook, Mr. Valdez, was usually available to take the ferry across the river when it was needed. Oldtimers recall the winter of 1918 when the Grassy Lake ferry was left in the water by mistake and went out with the ice the following spring.

Both ferries appear to have operated, according to the annual reports, until 1925.

GREGORY CROSSING FERRY
(1913-60)
Red Deer River   NW4-22-13-4

The first "ferry" at this crossing was a scow built and operated by Jim Gregory whose homestead was south of the river near the crossing. His scow's capacity was one team and a democrat, and he poled the scow across and downriver with the current. After crossing, it was then drawn back upstream by a team of horses before being poled to the other side again.

A government ferry was built and installed in 1913 as "Gregory's Ford," reputedly being operated first by H. B. Schofield and Bill Hosler. Like many other ferries, it became a popular gathering place for local residents and the crossing was the scene of many summer picnics.

There were many incidents at the Gregory Crossing ferry. About 1914, when it was loaded with show horses on their way to the Calgary Exhibition, it broke loose and went downriver for about ten miles, where luckily it hit the right bank for the horses to be unloaded. Two people were drowned in 1928 when a driver put his car into reverse gear in error, plunging the vehicle and its occupants into the river. In 1947, a big cattle herd was being taken to their summer range when they had to cross on the Gregory ferry, as the Emerson bridge was washed away before they could reach it. Also, one oldtimer recalled:

"On one occasion I went down to Gregory's Crossing on my way to Millicent and found a riderless horse standing, with his head down and reins hanging loose, on the opposite side of the river. I learned that his rider had attempted to ford the river by the side of the ferry, lost his seat, and was drowned." (Larry Helmer)

Winter crossings were made on the ice, and Larry Helmer recalled the day he arrived with a team and buggy in the late fall. The slush ice was still running and Larry had to sleep on the river bank in 10° below weather for five days until the ice was strong enough to cross.

The new Emerson bridge was opened in 1961 and users of the Gregory ferry were able to cross on this. The Gregory ferry, and also the ferryman's shack, were moved down to the Steveville crossing in the spring of 1961.

GROUARD FERRY
(1898-1901, 1908-15)
Lesser Slave Lake

This crossing, located on the narrows between Lesser Slave Lake and Buffalo Bay, was listed in the 1898 North-West Territorial Government report as one of three cable ferries "which have been provided by private individuals on the road from Edmonton to Peace River." (The other two were Belvedere and Fort Assiniboine-Holmes' Crossing). These were, no doubt, to accommodate the tremendous number of people rushing to the Klondike goldfields in that year. Like the other two ferries, it operated under a yearly licence with "a high schedule of tolls . . . for the purpose of giving settlers access to market." The Grouard ferry operated until 1901, when it was dropped from the North-West Territorial Government's report.

However, the little settlement of Grouard on the north shore of the narrows continued to grow, becoming an important stopping place for northbound travellers, and also the site of the Anglican and Catholic missions. As a result, it is likely that the ferry continued to operate after 1901.

In 1908, the provincial government installed a ferry which operated until a wooden trestle bridge was built in 1915. The old trail from Edmonton via Athabasca ran south of the ninety-mile Lesser Slave Lake, and between 1908 and 1915 many immigrants to the Peace River

103

country used the ferry to cross over to Grouard for supplies, or for a night's rest.

GROVEDALE FERRY
(1934-58)
Wapiti River   SW23-70-6-6

The area south of the Wapiti River, south-west of Grande Prairie, was once known only to the Indians, the trappers, and the occasional "Mountie" on patrol. It was scheduled as a protected area by the Dominion Government which ruled that no settlement would be allowed in the area in order to preserve its natural resources.

During the late 1920s and early 1930s, however, many settlers found their way into the area and established homesteads; they were looked upon as squatters with no actual rights to the land. Consequently, when they petitioned the provincial government for a ferry so that they could take their grain and livestock into Grande Prairie, their petitions were rejected as they were not officially supposed to be there.

However, early in the Depression, a federal inspector of surveys in the area agreed that the settlers could hardly be turned out at that stage, so the land was surveyed and the squatters were given the right to their land.

In 1933, local sawmill owner T. Cooke offered to build and operate a ferry, but his applications for a ferry licence were turned down. However, a ferry materialized in 1934 when local residents built roads and approaches on each side of the river, and a small ferry, about six feet shorter than the government ferries, was launched. A. H. McQuarrie, the provincial government road and ferry inspector, surveyed the ferry site and obtained a discarded ferry cable from the Dunvegan crossing, as well as material from one of the Smoky River ferries. He actually paid for the work on the ferry himself and was reimbursed by the government for only part of the cost.

Farmers and settlers willingly paid toll charges to cross on the ferry, and the annual reports described it from 1936 to 1941 as "S. of Grande Prairie — private ferry — paid operator." There is no indication who paid the ferryman — the government or the settlers — or whether he was just allowed to keep the toll charges. This private ferry appears to have continued to operate without formal permission, but it was under the aegis of the government, which built a new standard-sized ferry and installed it in 1940, when the name was changed to Grovedale Crossing.

By 1954 traffic had increased to the point where a petition was sent to the government by Grande Prairie residents to have the ferry operate twenty-four hours a day; this was done, with two operators on alternating eight-hour shifts.

A bridge was opened to traffic in 1958 and the Grovedale ferry was hauled by truck to a point south of Falher on the Little Smoky River for use there.

HAZEL BLUFF FERRY
(1912-16)
Pembina River   4/9-60-1-5

There appears to have been a shifting of ferries in this area between 1912 and 1916. The "West of Hazel Bluff" ferry, by which name it was listed in the annual reports for the five years it was in operation, seems to have been installed when the ferry from Lett's Crossing was moved a few miles upriver in 1912. Whether changes in settlement pattern or river conditions caused this shifting is not known.

There is no record of the ferryman at this crossing, unless it was an Andrew Jenner, whose name appears in the 1914 Alberta Gazeteer. A bridge at 9-60-1-5, built in 1916, saw the end of the West of Hazel Bluff ferry.

HEINSBURG FERRY
(1914-63)
North Saskatchewan River   SW22-55-4-4

After the Heinsburg post office was established in 1913 — named after first postmaster John Heins — a ferry was installed a year later to

The ferry across the North Saskatchewan River was an essential form of transportation for the people of Heinsburg. Established in 1914, the ferry is seen here in the 1930s.

serve the community. For almost fifty years it was operated at this busy crossing, being reclassified to Class A in 1929, with two ferrymen, sometimes three. The ferryman's shack was a small log cabin.

The ferry was used extensively in spring to transport herds of cattle to their summer ranges, with cows and calves sometimes jumping from or falling off the craft, with the resulting noise and chasing, roping and hauling back on deck. Farmers crossed to the railhead with their grain, livestock and cream, while holidays and weekends saw long lines of traffic waiting to cross for picnics at the lake.

The Heinsburg ferry had its share of accidents, too. In the flood waters of 1916, it broke loose and swept off downriver with the ferryman's wife on board. The ferryman at Lea Park, about ten miles downriver, saw the ferry coming down with the worried lady on deck, waving wildly and shouting "Never mind the ferry . . . save me!" The Heinsburg crossing was without ferry for the remainder of 1916, a new one being built and floated down from Edmonton for the spring of 1917.

In 1918, just at freeze-up time, four travellers arrived at the crossing in a Chevrolet, but with the ferry not operating and the ice not strong enough, they had to drive all the way to the nearest bridge at North Battleford — a trip of over a hundred miles which took them a week to make, instead of just a couple of hours if they had been able to cross at Heinsburg.

Another winter crossing involved a man who decided that the ice was strong enough to get him across in his Model T, so he drove over at a fast pace in the dark, not noticing that his car had dislodged a large chunk of newly-formed ice. On his return trip, the Model T went into the river where the chunk of ice had been, and sank with the driver in it. He was rescued, but the car, which could be seen on the river bottom with its lights still on, had to be hauled out later.

Several of the accidents at this crossing were fatal ones. Sometime in the early 1940s, when the river was exceptionally high, a young boy fell off the south landing ramp and was drowned, his body never being recovered. On another occasion, a young man from the St. Paul district was drowned while swimming; and in 1943, two young girls driving home with their boy friends from a dance were drowned after the car rolled off the ferry and sank in about twelve feet of water.

One early homesteader borrowed a horse from his son who lived across the river, turning it loose as soon as the job was done. The horse knew it had to get across the river to get home and tried for days to get on the ferry. The ferryman finally allowed it on and the horse reached home safely.

106

Buck Smith built this ferry on the Highwood River to carry traffic on the Calgary-Fort Macleod Trail. The owner was criticized for his outrageous fees.

In the early 1940s, local residents built a platform for crossing in spring and fall; it consisted of two long planks, some angle iron and two pulleys which they rigged up on the ferry cable. This could be moved across by passengers sitting on the platform and pulling themselves across by means of a long pole with a locking device on the end of it. This could be pushed along the cable and, when the pole was pulled back, the lock would tighten on the cable. A young farmer crossed in this way to take a large can of cream to the station, also to meet his wife and newborn baby off the train. On the return trip, his wife sat on the platform holding the baby with one arm, and the empty cream can with the other, while the husband pulled them all across.

A few years later the government installed a winter crossing "cage" with a motor and clutch. This was used, winter, spring and fall until the ferry service was discontinued.

Gilbert (Gib) Evans, local homesteader and a Justice of the Peace, operated the Heinsburg ferry for over twenty years altogether. He recalled gophers swimming across the river, sometimes riding on the ferry.

HIGH RIVER FERRY
(1886-?)
Highwood River

Jasper (Buck) Smith arrived in the High River area before 1880 and built a 1½-storey hotel by the river on the old Fort Benton Trail. The

107

The Hinton ferry spanned the Athabasca River but was moved ten times along an eight-mile stretch of river during its short lifetime. It is seen here about 1919.

bull teams went through and made the river crossing, wagon by wagon, a laborious process, until the arrival of the CPR in Calgary in 1883 ended the Benton traffic. in 1886, the one-eyed, poker-playing Smith built a ferry, reputedly with the help of famous black rancher, John Ware. The flat-bottomed scow, powered by cable and windlass, carried travellers across the river just a little upstream from the present CPR crossing. The ferry apparently remained in operation for several years as the NWMP annual report for 1889 refers to it, and to the need for a bridge at this point:

> There is a ferry at High River but the rates charged are high and it is a severe tax on settler pockets to have to use the ferry often.

HINTON FERRY
(1914-19 [1928?])
Athabasca River   SE¼-51-25-5

The provincial government installed a ferry "on the Athabasca River at Hinton (purchased) in 1914" but there are no records to indicate from whom it was purchased. The above location puts the ferry on the river just east of today's Highway 40, which adds to the confusion for, according to Bridge Branch records, there was a bridge there in 1913.

The government annual reports list the Hinton ferry until 1919, while another list indicates that it was in operation until 1928, although there is no mention of it in records between 1925 and 1928. With

108

official records for the period unavailable, the Hinton ferry remains a mystery, until further information comes to light. The fact that the location of old Hinton (formerly Prairie Creek) was moved ten times within eight miles, east to west along the river, may have something to do with the uncertain ferry operation.

HOLBORN FERRY
(1911-65)
North Saskatchewan River   27/28-50-1-5

This ferry was installed as "Lamora's Landing" and listed as such until 1916 when it became "Lamora's Crossing" until 1933, and then "S. of Holborn" from 1934 to 1965. Its true name was apparently meant to be "Lamoureaux Landing," but no reason for this name has been found so far, although it may have been named after an early settler.

Muriel Ducholke, daughter of a ferryman, tells the following story:

> We moved out to our homestead in 1917 [south of the crossing] . . . we really enjoyed the old ferry the years that Dad [J. Gibson] ran it. I spent many hours there and could operate it as well as he could . . . . we had many a picnic at the ferry in my happy childhood. One time Dad and I crossed when they were booming logs down from Rocky Mountain House and were stranded for about three hours in midstream, piking the logs away to keep them from swamping us, but even so, they turned the ferry at a sharp angle — a day I'll never forget. One fall, Dad and I crossed on the thin ice using a long plank. One spring a man broke through the ice with a steam engine which sank, all we could see was the smoke stack. Another time, at high water Dad took a man across with his team and wagon, with the horses unhitched so that they could swim if necessary. The ferry bobbed up and down, with the water up to the wagon axles, but he made the crossing. When the ferry was put in and taken out, I used to ride our horse [old Maud] round and round a winch on a cable to pull it out on skids of large peeled logs.

C. R. Meads of Stony Plain operated the ferry for about twenty-three years, followed by G. Meads; the latter family was represented for about half the period of the ferry's operation. The last ferryman before the Genesee bridge caused the ferry to be discontinued in 1965, reported only about six passengers per week during its last year or two, and then most of them seemed to find it by accident. Tormod Nesjan said that people from only a few miles south didn't even know a ferry was there.

HOLMES CROSSING FERRY
(1898-1900, 1905-56)
Athabasca River   E½-31-61-6-5

The earlier ferry at this crossing was built and operated privately under licence of the North-West Territorial Government, which listed it in its annual reports for 1898, 1899 and 1900 only. In 1898 it carried many goldseekers on their way to the Klondike and "the schedule of tolls was high as it was only used by freighters and persons travelling to the north country." This first crossing was on what was then called "the Edmonton-Peace River road," otherwise the famous Klondike Trail. Several accounts of the journey to the Klondike mention the ferry at this point, but all comments were reserved for the litter of broken boxes, smashed sleighs and harness on the long steep hill on the other side of the river, which put an end to the journey for many a goldseeker.

The ferry was not listed after 1900, but appeared in the report of the North-West Territorial Government as one of the ferries taken over by the new province in 1905.

William Holmes, a former camp cook, settled at the crossing in 1905 and made an attempt to get the old ferry into service again. In 1906, the provincial government moved the ferry to a site near "Billy" Holmes' homestead and appointed him as the ferryman, a job he held for about seven years. Billy was also the local postmaster and as the little settlement grew it came to be known as Holmes' Crossing. Over the years traffic increased considerably and in the 1940s the ferry transported several million feet of lumber every year. It was even part of the route for the Barrhead to Fort Assiniboine bus service.

Local history records the story of an early settler who fired thirty rounds of ammunition to try to rouse the ferryman to take him and his pregnant wife across to the doctor at the town, but the ferryman slept extra soundly that night and the baby had to make its entrance into the world at home, without the help of the doctor.

A sad accident took place in 1949 when three men in a car (also loaded with bottles of beer) drove onto the ferry at high speed in top gear with no brakes, and right off the other end. All three men were drowned.

Spring and fall were difficult times for river crossings, so a wooden, crate-like conveyance was rigged up to carry passengers, mail and supplies across — but no livestock, lumber or heavy loads.

Wesley Cartwright was the ferryman here for about twenty years, and a story is told of him suffering some broken ribs when trying to take some horses across. This may have been the time when Jack Rea (later an employee of Glenbow Museum), had occasion to cross about seventy-five head of horses. It took a long time to persuade the frightened animals to approach the ferry, but when they got the first few on deck all the rest followed, and the ferry sank!

110

HOPKINS CROSSING FERRY
(1908-70)
North Saskatchewan River   5/6-56-7-4

Local Dominion Land Surveyor Marshall Willard Hopkins surveyed the St. Paul area of the province about 1903-04, and the post settlement of Hopkins was named after him in 1908 when the post office was established at the Trading Store. A ferry was installed in 1908 to enable farmers to cross the river to the railway, and although the post office was discontinued in 1915, the ferry continued to operate as "Hopkins" until 1970, when the bridge at Myrnam was opened. It was a busy crossing in the early years as it was the only ferry on the river in that area, until the Mooswa (Lindbergh) ferry was installed in 1911. The Hopkins ferry apparently operated safely and satisfactorily during its sixty-two years of service as there is no record of any serious mishaps; although it probably had its share of trouble due to high water periods and winter ice crossings.

One day in 1916 when the water was running high, a barn was seen floating down the river with three Jersey cows still inside. The ferryman, with a couple of helpers, took the ferry out into midstream, hoping to block the barn's journey, but they were just a few feet out and the barn merely glanced off the ferry and went on its way, the three cows staring ahead calmly.

On another occasion, someone tried to cross a herd of horses on the ice in winter, well strung out to that their weight would not break the ice. Unluckily, when they were halfway across, the ice "boomed," as it often did when freezing, and the horses took fright and bunched together, all being drowned when the ice collapsed under their weight.

Leon Kobel, the last ferryman at Hopkins, spent a total of twenty-five years altogether in this job.

HOUK FERRY
(c. 1880s-1890s)
St. Mary's River

George Houk was one of the first ranchers on the east side of the St. Mary's River south of present-day Lethbridge, where he ran a stopping house, providing meals and beds for travellers, and he also built and operated a cable ferry. George came to Canada from Montana about 1866, panned for gold in the Edmonton and Peace River districts, and returned to southern Alberta about 1870, helping to build a new Fort Hamilton (Whoop-Up) after the old one had been burned to the ground.

The Houk ferry carried many early travellers and emigrants from the United States, as well as all the I. G. Baker bull teams bringing supplies up to Canada from Fort Benton, Montana. After the narrow-gauge "Turkey Trail" railway to Dunmore from Coal Banks (Lethbridge) was completed in 1885, traffic on the ferry diminished somewhat until the arrival of Charles Ora Card and his followers from Utah in 1887, and the little community of Cardston was established. The ferry again saw increased traffic as the residents of Cardston used it on their journeys to Lethbridge. Charles Ora Card's diary for 17 June, 1890, states that:

> On the way from Cardston to Lethbridge we ferried the wagons and forded the horses . . . . I went to Mr. Houks and hired a bed for the night.

In 1888, the Layton family arrived in the area and homesteaded close to the river. Mr. Layton was attracted by the Houk ferry so after he proved up his homestead, he bought the ferry from George Houk, moved to the crossing and operated it until about 1892. James Myron Layton Jr. recalled the Houk ferry as being an attraction to local people who would stand and watch all the freight teams crossing. The crossing itself, with shelter and wood available on both sides of the river, was always busy as it was a good place to camp overnight on the three-day journey from Cardston to Lethbridge or the return trip.

A steel bridge was built over the river at Cardston in 1894, but the Houk ferry continued to serve traffic between Lethbridge and the settlements up the Belly River, including Standoff and the St. Mary's North-West Mounted Police post. There is no record as to when the ferry ceased to operate.

HUTTON FERRY
(1908-60)
Red Deer River   NE6-24-14-4

The ferry installed by the government in 1908 was about two miles downriver from the above location, at the little post settlement of Fieldholme, where George Field, an early settler, ran a stopping house and post office at his ranch. Field and his brother operated the ferry during its early years of operation, when it was one of the busiest on the river. Fieldholme was the mail centre for the district and was also a stopping place for the stagecoach service operated by Colonel Felix Warren (reputedly a friend of Buffalo Bill Cody), between Bassano and Richdale.

The ferry was listed in the annual reports as Fieldholme from 1908 to 1923, but there is no record of the actual date of its removal upriver to the Hutton townsite. It was about 1911 when Baldwin P. Hutton, manager of the Northern Crown Bank in Calgary, staked out a town-

Farm wagons with settlers' effects are lined up waiting for the Hutton ferry to cross the Red Deer River in 1913.

site of about 600 lots about two miles upriver from the Fieldholme ferry. It was named Hutton and visualized by its promoters, the Hutton Townsite Company, as a major business centre, a rival to Calgary. However, by 1920 it was reduced to a few derelict buildings, with the name of Hutton being dropped from the maps of Alberta. Nevertheless, the ferry's name was changed to Hutton in the 1924 annual report, and remained under this name until it was discontinued in 1960 when the Duchess bridge was built on highway 36.

One of the early ferrymen was the well-known "Irish" Mellon who had previously run the old Blue Rock Hotel in Calgary. Another ferryman apparently came to a very sad end as he was found frozen to death one winter while still living in the ferryman's shack. His faithful dog was by his side, so attached to his master that he had to be destroyed.

Local history tells the story of a homesteader taking a steam tractor across on the ferry about 1912, when both ferry and tractor sank. It took about a week to get them both out of the river.

IDDESLEIGH FERRY
(1913-24)
Red Deer River   2-21-11-4
The Iddesleigh ferry was installed in 1913 as "Dead Lodge Canyon," by which name it was listed in the annual reports until 1916, then

113

changed to Iddesleigh, or "W. of Iddesleigh." It was located in the present Dinosaur Provincial Park on what was then Hansel G. (Happy Jack) Jackson's homestead.

Although there are no available records of ferrymen prior to 1924, there is written evidence that Happy Jack did, perhaps, act as the ferryman, or the assistant ferryman at some time during its operation. It is referred to in many historical notes as the "Jackson Ferry," and Happy Jack's diaries, in his own handwriting (now in the Glenbow Museum in Calgary) indicate that he did have a hand in its operation. For instance:

28 March 1915 — "Put the ferry in"
3 April 1915 — "The ferry sank"
12 April 1915 — "Put the ferry in"

and so, throughout the years, until at least 1920, the diary contains many references to the ferry going in and out.

Whether or not Jackson was the ferryman, he met many travellers on it. Local residents gathered at the ferry for summer picnics and Jackson, with his big moustache and Stetson hat, he was well liked by all who met him.

The Jenner ferry was established in 1914 so that farmers could reach the railhead. It is a lonely isolated spot, so the ferryman probably welcomed any travellers.

114

JARVIE FERRY
(1930s & 1944)
Pembina River

The bridge at Jarvie was taken out by flood waters sometime in the 1930s, part of it going as far south as the mouth of the Pembina River. The replacement bridge was taken out again in 1944 when debris from upriver piled up against it, resulting in its collapse. One span ended up six miles downriver in a field. On both occasions a ferry was put into service until the bridges were rebuilt.

JENNER FERRY
(1914-81)
Red Deer River   W½2-22-9-4

Originally named Websdale, the post office was opened in 1913 to serve the growing number of settlers in the area, and the village which was located at 20-9-4 was subsequently named Jenner, apparently after famous English physician, Dr. Edward Jenner (1749-1823). A ferry was installed in 1914 to enable farmers to reach the railhead. It was about eight miles north of the village on the present Highway 884. A lonely spot, a means of crossing the river, it was never the hub of a community.

Apparently its service was helpful and taken for granted, but uneventful. Even by the 1930s the crossing was still isolated and as the river level fluctuated somewhat during the summer months, shifting sandbars sometimes hampered the ferry's operation.

In 1931 a bridge was built at Buffalo on Highway S886 and heavier traffic could go around that way, although this meant a journey of many more miles to the railway. In later years, increased traffic and trucks carrying heavy equipment between Suffield and Youngstown proved to be too much for the little ferry, so a bridge was built and opened to traffic in 1981. A new scow had been provided in 1979, the old ferry being preserved at the Table Rock Rodeo grounds about three hundred yards from the crossing. The newer ferry was taken north to serve as a temporary crossing in 1982 when the bridge at Elk Point on the North Saskatchewan River was burned.

KINUSO FERRY
(1912)
Swan River   73-10-5

A ferry was apparently installed at the above location in 1912, which would put it in the general vicinity of Kinuso. The ferry was not mentioned in any of the annual reports but only on a general list so there is no indication how long it operated, if indeed it was ever there at all.

A man and his team were drowned while trying to cross the river near Kinuso in 1919, and shortly after that the Kinuso postmaster petitioned the government for a ferry to be installed at 7/8-72-9-5, just south of Kinuso, as there were about fifteen children who were unable to cross the river to attend school. The petition, however, was not successful. It is possible that the 1912 ferry was on the old trail from Edmonton to High Prairie, used by many early pioneers.

KLONDYKE FERRY
(1931-83)
Athabasca River   11-63-4-5

Construction of the "Klondyke" ferry (so named because the crossing was on the overland route to the goldfields in 1898) was begun in 1931 and completed and the ferry put in service in 1932 at a total cost of about $3,000. It was known locally as "Fowler's Crossing" after the first ferryman, G. J. (Jim) Fowler, of Vega.

It was always a busy little ferry, carrying local farmers and residents as well as farm machinery, saddle horses and livestock, and was one of the few remaining ferries in the province until the spring of 1983, when it was replaced by a modern bridge. The ferry had other uses: in the early 1940s, it was used as a baptismal site, participants in the ceremonies being immersed in the water from the ferry's deck; it has also been the scene of square dances, held on the ferry's deck. The early pioneers and today's residents have crossed the ferry to gather wild blueberries for jam and pies. Winter crossings are made on the ice. In the early 1940s, one ferryman, Horace Sebern made a boat with runners on it to cross before the ice was strong enough to walk on.

"LA COREY" FERRY
(1915-26?)
Beaver River   6-25-62-6-4

This is "mystery" ferry which was shown on provincial government lists, located just about where the present bridge crosses the river on Highway 890, south of La Corey. According to local historian, Anatole Mercier, a bridge was built at SE25-62-6-4 in 1916, and he thought that perhaps the ferry was installed there in 1915 for use by the bridge crew. However, the government list showed it operating until 1926, so it may be the ferry on which Frank Levesque acted as ferryman. According to his son, John, Frank built a home on the river bank in 1913, and he afterwards "ran the ferry across the Beaver River . . . until 1921."

Whatever the story, a photograph proves that the ferry existed.

116

LA CRETE FERRY
(1961-present)
Peace River   30/31-103-19-5

When a new ferry was built for the Fort Vermilion crossing in 1961, the old ferry from that location was taken up river to Tompkins Landing, between Paddle Prairie and La Crete to provide a shorter route for truckers, timber haulers, and farmers seeking a market in the south. All had previously used the unimproved road between Fort Vermilion and Peace River. The ferry, listed in the annual reports as the La Crete ferry, cut short the journey by about 160 miles.

In the winters an ice bridge was made, but during spring and fall river conditions made the crossing at Tompkins Landing impassable. Viewed as a low cost alternative to building a $10 million bridge at the crossing, it was decided to experiment with a modern hoverferry, which was designed by Hoverlift Systems Ltd. in Calgary and assembled in Edmonton by Central Fabricators Ltd. The hoverferry, designed to ride on a cushion of air, guided by cables, would be able to ride over ice ridges $2\frac{1}{2}$ feet high and it was hoped that it would provide year round operation both on the ice and in spring and fall slush ice conditions. It would carry, on its 66-foot long deck, seven or eight cars or a large 100,000-pound truck, a weight capacity of thirty-five to fifty tons, and would operate on two engines. It would also be tested for possible use over muskeg, swamps and lakes.

Christened "Pioneer I," the new hoverferry was launched on its maiden voyage on 5 October 1977. About five hundred local residents, including children who had been given the day off school, lined up on the river banks to watch the launching which was attended by cabinet ministers, officials and guests. There was a champagne christening, sandwiches, coffee and soft drinks available to all. The ferry was winched across the stretch of water with all the officials and guests on board. As it neared the opposite bank one of the rubber aprons which traps the cushion of air lifted and sprayed the passengers with dollops of mud, the president of Hoverlift Systems Ltd. reportedly receiving most of it. On its return journey the craft zigzagged slowly through the water, the slack cables not being properly adjusted. However, officials proclaimed the maiden voyage satisfactory but admitted that there appeared to be many kinks to be ironed out.

Tests, including operating conditions, weight capacity tests and speed trials, were to continue for two years, the old cable ferry being retained at the crossing as a standby. Many of the original kinks were ironed out, but more appeared. The gleaming new hoverferry which had brought the twentieth century to once peaceful Tompkins Landing was still hampered by problems, mainly inadequate winches, and

117

Mrs. L. O. Crockett is seen crossing the narrows on the Lac Ste. Anne ferry in the summer of 1913. Next in line is Bill Armstrong from the Holden district.

even after a year, it was still classed as "experimental," with operating costs rising rapidly although the air blast was found to be a good ice breaker.

Some local residents, who had been asking for better roads, water and sewer systems, hospital services, and more homestead land, expressed their disapproval at being presented with a "new-fangled" hovercraft, and felt that it would never replace the old cable ferry. They were right. Problems caused by the winch and the spray skirt, not to mention the river, which, in a most unusual manner formed an ice jam so large, rough and high that the hovercraft could not clear it, finally caused the modern craft to be withdrawn altogether. It just goes to prove that "Nature, not Man, is the boss." The old ferry returned to service and is still operating.

LAC STE. ANNE FERRY
(1906, 1908-62)
Lac Ste. Anne

David Thompson used its Indian name of "Manito Lake" in 1796, but in 1844 when the Roman Catholics built a mission there, it was changed to Lac Ste. Anne. There is no record of any ferry on the lake, however, until 1906 when the Rev. J. B. Bickersteth passed this way and wrote in his book, *Land of Open Doors,* that

> . . . on April 18, 1906 a stagecoach service was established between Lac Ste. Anne and Edmonton. The same month it became a cinch to cross over the Narrows because the ferry started operating there.

This earlier ferry must have been the crude raft on empty coal oil barrels operated by an old Stoney Indian, known locally as "Weezaw"

118

— no doubt a corruption of *oiseau,* the French word for bird. The raft was pulled back and forth across Buffalo Bay Narrows by means of a rope fastened to both ends. "Weezaw" had several Indian women doing the pulling while he bossed the operation. The women caught the rope at the front end of the raft and walked to the rear, pulling the raft across by sheer muscle power. The charge to cross was twenty-five cents.

The provincial government installed a ferry in 1908 and this was, like other lake ferries, operated by a rope or cable wound in a drum turned over by a crank. The ferry was operated for many years in this way — a hand propelled crank — but a small gasoline engine was installed in 1957 to make the crossing a bit easier. The ferry was run for many years by two brothers, Hugh and Ernie Jones, two bachelors who homesteaded on the south bank. Hugh had been a chemist in his native Wales at one time, and besides operating the ferry he treated the ailments of the Indians on the Alexis Reserve. Ernie was a fine singer and journeyed to Salt Lake City on occasion to sing in a Welsh choir there.

LEA PARK FERRY
(1908-57)
North Saskatchewan River   14-54-3-4

In the early 1800s the Hudson's Bay Company and the North West Company built trading posts just north of the river at this crossing. Indians and fur traders forded the river just east of the confluence of the Vermilion and North Saskatchewan Rivers until both posts were abandoned about 1810.

With the arrival of settlers in the area after the turn of the century, a post office and store were established on the south bank of the river and the settlement named Lea Park, allegedly after Tom and Bill Lea, two of the first settlers. At this time the little town of Kitscoty to the south was the nearest point where farmers could sell produce and buy groceries, so a ferry was installed in 1908. It was listed as "N. of Kitscoty" by which name it was shown in the annual reports until 1923, changing to Lea Park in 1924.

The ferry was used extensively for crossing cattle herds in the spring and fall, as many community and private pastures were located north of the river. Crossing cattle in herds was always a problem. First they would have to be driven or persuaded on to the ferry, but some might jump off halfway across the river. These would be followed by the rest of the herd on deck and they would sometimes swim the wrong way, back to where they started. The resulting round-ups stretched the tempers of all concerned and the sounds of swearing were mingled with the mooing and bawling of the cattle. On one occasion, the ferry, overloaded with cattle, sank in midstream but all swam safely to shore. One cattle buyer who lived at Mooswa (Lindbergh) used to travel from farm to farm buying cattle and then drive them all to the ferry for transportation to Kitscoty.

Bill Katherens, a Ferry Inspector, recalled that the water and current conditions at Lea Park were the best that the ferry crews ever had to deal with. He also told of a spring launching when the steel rollers underneath the ferry slipped and caused it to veer sideways, breaking two of the planks on the bottom. Jack Timblin, another Ferry Inspector, used his wide vocabulary of swear words in venting his wrath on the ferryman who let this happen. Jack repaired the ferry and prepared to take charge of the launching himself — and the very same thing happened again!

Apparently there was only one fatal accident during the ferry's years of service. Ferryman "Swan" Johnson (Sven Johanson) was drowned while trying to rescue his small son, Clarence, who had fallen into the river. Swan's body was found some time later by the ferryman at Hewitt's Landing about 25 miles east, but the boy's body never turned up.

On one occasion, two Model T's drove down the hill, one behind the other, and both ended up in the river with just their tops showing, but all the occupants managed to swim to shore. One local farmer left his team of two oxen outside the store on the south bank but old Tom and Jerry decided to keep on going and ambled down to the ferry, onto the deck, and right off the other side. The oxen were rescued after being cut out of the harness in which they were entangled.

The first ferryman at Lea Park was Louis Patenaude, a Metis who had taken part in the 1885 Rebellion; he was remembered as being a friendly and efficient ferryman. Ed Klinkner was a ferryman in the 1940s; it was Ed whose pet gander used to ride back and forth on the ferry with him. Ole Tweed, another ferryman, was threatened with a lawsuit by an irate man who drove his car off the end of the ferry, having failed to obey Ole's orders on disembarking. Ole, incidentally, produced his own very good "dark ale," which some of the local ladies did not approve of their husbands sharing!

The Lea Park bridge was opened to traffic in 1958 by the Minister of Highways, who was presented with a little doll named "Little Miss Ferryboat" in memory of the Lea Park ferry which had served the crossing for almost fifty years.

This 1883 photographs show Nicholas Sheran's ferry on the Oldman River at Coalbanks, later Lethbridge. Sheran's shack and mining operation was on the opposite bank.

LETHBRIDGE FERRY
(ca. 1872-1904)
Oldman River

The site of Coal Banks (Lethbridge) was determined by the availability of its coal deposits and not, as was the case with other river settlements, because it was close to a shallow ford for easy crossing. What fords there were at this point were under steep river banks, and the lives of many men and horses were lost when trying to cross the river.

A wandering Irish-American soldier and adventurer, Nicholas Sheran, who joined notorious whisky traders Healy and Hamilton at old Fort Hamilton (Fort Whoop-Up), operated a small ferry there. In his spare time, Sheran roamed up and down the river banks where he discovered coal in large quantities and started the first underground mining at what came to be known as Coal Banks. His ferry crossing was known by several names — Coal Banks (Lethbridge), Coal Hurst, Sheran's Crossing, and Sheran's Ferry.

About 1880, missionary John Maclean noted in his diary:

> We hailed Nick Sheran . . . who was the ferryman with his rowboat on the occasions when his services were required. With 11 wagons and 27 horses, 7 hours were consumed in crossing the river, as all the waggons had to be taken to pieces and ferried over in the small boat.

121

Sheran was drowned at the Kipp ferry in 1882 and a year later a ferry was built and installed at Coal Banks by the Alberta Coal & Navigation Company, owned by the Galt family. However, it was not very satisfactory, the ferry approaches being too steep. According to all reports, this ferry was nearly always out of commission, either because of low or high water, spring and fall conditions, or because of the cable breaking and the ferry being swept downriver.

A bridge was built and opened to traffic in 1899, but even the approaches to the bridge were very steep and a single team had difficulty in pulling even an empty wagon up the grades.

The ferry remained in operation until 1904 until the bridge, which was washed away in 1902, had been rebuilt and the approaches levelled so that all traffic could use it.

LETT'S CROSSING FERRY
(1908-12, 1913-15 & 1925-65)
Pembina River   10-60-1-5, 23-60-1-5

The ferry was originally installed in 1908 as "Pembina," the settlement of that name being incorporated in 1906 with G. H. Letts as the first postmaster. It was located at 10-60-1-5 was moved to 23-60-1-5 in 1913. In 1915, the year when many ferries were damaged by floods, it was not shown on the annual report, except a brief note that it "was discontinued." It was not listed thereafter until 1919 when "a new ferry was built." It appeared on the 1920 report, but disappeared again until 1925, when "it was necessary to build   .   .   . new scow at Pembina." It appeared as "Lett's Crossing" in 1926 and thereafter until 1965, its last year of operation. It was also referred to in some later government files as the "Riverdale" ferry. A small one-room shack was also built by the government in 1926 for the ferrymen to use during the summer months.

During its years of operation the ferry provided a more direct route to the railway for farmers west of the river and it was also used by children crossing to the Riverdale school.

The ferryman in 1926 and 1927 was the locally well-known "Jockie" Calder. Scott Durling owned the land adjacent to the ferry and he took over as the ferryman in 1935 to replace G. W. Kidney, who died that year. Mrs. Durling recalled the sad occasion when a three-year-old girl was drowned in the river, as did a lady who walked out from Westlock. There were also many near drownings in the summertime when the river near the crossing was filled with swimmers.

One joyful event recalled by Mrs. Durling was the birth of a baby boy in the ferryman's shack in the 1940s. Ferryman Bill Tennant hammered on Mrs. Durling's door one day, scared that he might have to act as midwife for a lady whose husband could not get their horses up the slippery hill to the doctor at Westlock after crossing on the ferry. Much to Bill's relief, however, Mrs. Durling took over until the baby was safely delivered.

In 1946 and again in 1953, a rowboat had to be used for crossings as low water and sandbars hampered the ferry's operation. Bill Katherens, the Ferry Inspector, reported that the "scow was very heavy," which probably meant that it was getting waterlogged.

LINDBERGH FERRY
(1911-63)
North Saskatchewan River   E½-22-56-5-4

This crossing was the site of the old Moose Telegraph Station, installed in 1896 on the line from Edmonton to Battleford. Early settlers in the area chose the name "Tyrol" for the first post office established in 1910, but when this was moved in 1911, the name changed to "Mooswa." It was known by this name until 1928, when it was changed to "Lindbergh," reportedly in honour of Charles Lindbergh, the American aviator. By 1911, with more settlers, a store and a post office, a means of river crossing became a necessity and local residents with their teams of oxen worked hard to build a road down to the river. There was great excitement one spring day in 1911 when the telegraph station received the message that a ferry, built in Edmonton, was on its way down river.

Archie Pasmore and John Chilabeck went down with their horses to pull it to shore when it arrived. It was soon connected to the cable and put into service, to the great benefit of local residents who had previously used the Hopkins ferry about twenty miles upriver. At that time, the railroad was at Kitscoty, to the south, and the ferry was used to transport grain and livestock across the river. Cattle drives were organized for shipping via Islay to the ferry crossing, where the ferryman undertook the arduous task of ferrying them all across — some on the ferry, some swimming behind it. These drives usually took place in the fall after the trees had lost their leaves so that runaway cattle could more easily be seen and brought back to the herd. Winter crossings were made on the ice, but there is no record as to how spring and fall crossings were accomplished.

Nora Omness Ronaghan Williamson tells a story of the time she had to cross at the ferry crossing in 1918 after attending a dance at Ferguson Flats. When she reached the crossing after sliding down the long hill on her horse, she could see that the ice was already melting. She told her horse, "Shady, it's up to you to get me across." He very carefully tiptoed over the trail, which could just be seen across the ice, with trickles of water closing in behind him. Close to the opposite shore he broke through the ice and, after making several lunges to force his way through the slush, he finally regained his footing and got Nora out on to the river bank.

They were both soaked with the icy water and the ferryman, who had been watching their perilous journey, put a blanket over Shady, who was trembling with cold and exhaustion. Nora's clothes were dried by the fire in the ferryman's shack and he gave her a piece of bread thickly spread with butter and honey. As they watched the progress of melting water over the ice, they realized what a close call it had been.

LUNNFORD FERRY
(1910?-1925)
Pembina River   22-59-2-5

Early settler, E. L. Lunn, settled in this area prior to 1909 where he also ran a little store and, after the post office was incorporated in 1911, became its first postmaster. Customers coming to the east bank of the river had to attract the storekeeper's attention and would then be rowed across the river to the store and back again with their purchases. Mr. Lunn went to Scotland in 1909 and returned in 1910, which was apparently the year when a ferry was installed at the site, known locally as "Lunn's Ford." The Rev. Oswin Creighton, son of the Bishop of London, on a four-year missionary stay in Canada, crossed on the Lunnford ferry in 1910 and met Mr. Lunn. He noted that "the ferry had just been installed on the main trail from Edmonton to Peace River."

The government's annual report of 1910 indicates the movement of a ferry "from West of Wabamun" to a point on the Pembina known as Hood's Crossing, but as no other reference to this particular crossing has been found, it is not known whether this was, in fact, Lunnford or Sunniebend, which also saw a ferry installed in 1910. Local history states that the Lunnford Ferry was actually constructed at Belvedere and floated along to Lunnford.

The Lunnford ferry is not listed in the annual reports after 1925. The bridge at Lunnford, according to the Bridge Branch records, was opened in 1926. "Jockie" Calder, a former scout and interpreter during the Riel Rebellion of 1885, was the ferryman at Lunnford for several years.

McKENZIE FERRY
(1883-88)
Red Deer River

When Roderick and David McKenzie established a sawmill on the

124

river north-east of the Red Deer settlement in 1883, they also built and operated their own ferry. It was still in operation in 1886 when Roderick was engaged in freighting between Calgary and Edmonton, but in 1887 it apparently became swamped on a gravel bar in the river. It was put back into service but sank again in 1888 when its cable became entangled in a tree. Whether it was salvaged or not is not recorded, but it was purchased by Lewis Martin Sage in 1890 (see Cash City Ferry).

McLEOD VALLEY FERRY
(1912-54)
McLeod River   2-55-14-5

First installed as "North of Peers," by which name it was officially listed until 1923, this ferry was used mainly by farmers to bring their grain across to the railway. In the 1930s it was also used by employees of the McLeod River Mining Company and was designated as a Class A ferry, with two ferrymen, in 1938.

It was one of the ferries which apparently operated satisfactorily through the years. Mrs. Martha Samis, now of Bon Accord, tells the story of a beautiful chestnut stallion corralled near the ferry crossing which jumped its fence and swam after the ferry which was carrying a team of mares, determined to meet the "ladies." The stallion's owner had to row out in a small boat to capture it.

Bill Katherens, the Ferry Foreman (1936-1960), mentions in his memoirs that one of the ferrymen at this crossing in the early 1940s was an amputee, having lost both legs in a railroad accident.

McNEIL FERRY
(ca. 1920-?)
Belly River

Although not a ferry per se, Ed McNeil owned and operated a large, heavy rowboat which he used to ferry customers across the river to his store at Standoff when high water prevented teams and saddle horses from crossing.

McNeil ran a small store and post office on the north side of the river, adjacent to the Blood Indian Reserve. The little "ferry" — painted blue and named the "Betty Bumps" after one of Ed's granddaughters — was attached to a rope stretched between two stout posts on either side of the river. It was used by settlers and Indians to cross to the store for supplies. Ed hung an empty oil drum on a tree across the river and people would bang on it when they wanted to cross.

On treaty days, when the Indians received their money, the ferry would be kept busy and Ed would brew a large boiler of tea and open a large tin of sweet biscuits for his customers.

The ferry was in use only for a few years, until most of the customers had automobiles to drive around on the nearest bridge.

Just a short distance north of the McNeil store there was a contraption known as the "bucket" ferry, apparently some kind of metal container slung on a cable between two trees or posts for the purpose of transporting supplies across the river.

MAHASKA FERRY
(1918-53)
McLeod River   SE4-57-13-5

The post office settlement of Mahaska was named by early homesteaders from an Iowa county bearing the name of a 19th century Indian chief. In 1918 a ferry was installed where the 15th base line crossed the river. Harry Hellekson, the ferryman in 1925, recalled working on the ferry approaches when he and Pat Desjarlais were assigned the job of digging holes for the deadmen on each side of the river.

The first ferryman, Tom Fallon, was a little hard of hearing so he trained his dog to bark when someone wanted to cross on the ferry.

All the early ferrymen suffered from rain coming in through the sod roof of the ferryman's shack. A new one was finally built, but not until sometime in the 1930s.

Although this ferry was in operation for forty-five years, it saw very little traffic. At one time there was so little to do that the ferryman, in order to dispel his loneliness, rode to the top of the hill with each rig which crossed on the ferry. This enabled him to catch up on all the local news before he walked back to his lonely job.

MAJEAU LAKE FERRY
(1936-37)
Lake Majeau

The creek draining into Majeau Lake from the hills in the south flooded all the surrounding land in 1936 so Torvald Nelson built and operated a little "ferry." It was used in 1936 and 1937 only, the provincial government paying Nelson a small salary for his services.

The area west and south of the lake was not homesteaded to any great extent until the late 1920s and early 1930s, and consequently the roads at that time were very poor. The base line was the main road and having half a mile of it flooded posed quite a problem.

The main source of income for many of the local settlers was the cream which they sold to Edmonton creameries. The truck which came in from Edmonton every Monday morning met the farmers at "Grandpa Nels" Nelson's blacksmith yard on the east side of the meadow. Many cans of cream were therefore carried in Torvald's

126

Mrs. "Scotty" Welch prepares to cross the Oldman River on a home made "Mary Jane" ferry.

little flat-bottomed rowboat. It also transported the teachers to the Greenhill school, which the Nelsons had been largely instrumental in getting started, and carried the eagerly awaited library books from the circulating library sent out from Edmonton.

When travellers wished to cross the flooded meadow, they signalled to Mr. Nelson by raising a large, square "flag" made out of white flour sacking. They would lean the flagpole gainst Grandpa Nelson's porch where it could easily be seen against the black roof of the house. Frequent checks were made from the ferry to see if the flag was showing, but even so, travellers sometimes had enough time to drink several cups of coffee in Grandma Nelson's kitchen before the ferry got across for them.

In 1937, Torvald Nelson set up a buzzer system for signalling his ferry. This was battery-operated and the barbed wire fence conducted the current across the meadow. It was quite an improvement on the "flag" system.

MANOLA FERRY
(1910-27)
Pembina River   22-59-2-5

The little post settlement of Manola, named after Manola McFee, a daughter of the first postmistress, was established in 1907. The first settlers had come into the area about 1905, and in 1906 many more came up from California, causing it to be known as the "California settlement." By 1910, with two sawmills and a school, Wilbur Clarke built a ferry on his land near his homestead and he and Fred Ransome carried passengers across the river. Clarke's ferry was located about one mile downriver from the present bridge. After a road was built in 1912, more and more people settled in the area, and in 1913 the provincial government put in its own ferry in the vicinity of the present bridge. This was listed on the annual reports until 1927, with the exception of 1916 when it was probably one of the many ferries damaged in the 1915 floods.

"MARY JANE" FERRY
Oldman River

The "Mary Jane" plank ferry appears to have been a home made contraption for crossing the river near Lethbridge. According to Ms. Kaye Welch, the family "moved to an island east [sic] of town [Lethbridge]." There appears to have been a large sand bar west of the town in the early days — perhaps the "Mary Jane" was built and used for crossing to this. It does not seem to be like the cable cars used by the Federal Water Survey board, although there were a great number of these in the area.

Teams and wagons wait patiently to cross the South Saskatchewan River at Medicine Hat about 1907. The ferry wharf was about 150 yards from 1st Street SE.

128

MATTHEWS CROSSING FERRY
(1914-38)

Pembina River   13-54-7-5

The ferry from Entwistle, according to the annual report, was moved to this post office settlement in 1914. M. H. Matthews was the postmaster and also the first ferryman. The ferry was in operation for about twenty-four years.

MEDICINE HAT FERRY
(ca. 1883-1907)

South Saskatchewan River

On arriving at Medicine Hat [1883] we found a ferry in operation with Willing . . . in charge . . . he told me that . . . the engineer and some of the NWMP officers at Calgary and Macleod had formed a small company and had put in a ferry here and another one at Calgary. (*Tales of a Pioneer Surveyor* — Charles Aeneas Shaw.)

The North-West Mounted Police, who had moved to new barracks at Medicine Hat, reported that there was a "police ferry boat on the river." They are credited with ownership in spite of the fact that they, as government employees, could not profit by any commercial venture. Two reference sources, however, refer to lawyer James Lougheed as the owner and operator of the Medicine Hat ferry, so it is possible that it was operated under his name.

The crossing was about where 4th Avenue & 1st Street is today; the police appointed a man by the name of Long Day to operate it as a toll ferry. Day apparently pocketed all the tolls, to the annoyance of the police, who could take no action as the man threatened to report them to Ottawa for their interest in the financial venture.

The North-West Police annual reports for 1886 to 1894 mentioned the Medicine Hat ferry:

This ferry has always been a constant source of expense and annoyance . . . . I think it would be cheaper to sell the ferry outright or lease it to some competent person and have an established rate for crossing . . . foot passengers can go either by the bridge or rowboat. (Supt. Antrobus, November 1886)

This ferry was repaired at considerable expense . . . a substantial tower built and cable well stretched . . . the boat has been running well. (Supt. McIlree, November 1887)

The [ferry] belongs to the police and is managed by one of our own men. (Annual Reports, 1888 and 1889)

The police ferry at Medicine Hat has been repaired, a new lifeboat built, and is in [good] working order.

This ferry, no longer of much use to the police, is of great service to the few settlers who reside on the north side of the river. (1892)

In 1898, the first report of the North-West Territorial Government's Department of Public Works listed the ferry as being owned by the government, and it remained in their annual reports until 1905, when it was taken over by the new provincial government. During the period 1898 to 1905, there was considerable controversy as to whether the ferry should be taken over by the Town of Medicine Hat. In spite of petitions and arguments, including many long letters to the local newspaper by local ranchers who felt that it should be a free ferry, it apparently remained in operation as a government-owned toll ferry until 1905.

In 1898, a $5.00 ticket was good for fifty ferry trips. In 1899 the cost was doubled, to $10 for fifty trips. In 1901 the tickets cost $5.00 for twenty-four trips, or $10 for forty-eight trips. In the summer of 1905, with "traffic over the ferry very large and the boat running continuously" there was a sad accident when A. W. Green's horse and rig backed off the ferry. His baby son was thrown into the river and in trying to save him, Mr. Green drowned.

The ferry operated as a free service after 1905 and when a traffic bridge was built in 1908, the ferry was floated upriver to a point near Bow Island to serve as a crossing there.

MERIDIAN FERRY
(1910-20, 1921-24, 1925-present)
North Saskatchewan River   25-53-1-4, 5-53-28-3, 25-53-28-5

The ferry at this crossing was originally installed by the Alberta government in 1910 as "between Onion Lake & Lloydminster." In 1912 it was listed as "Near 4th," and from 1913 to 1918 as "4th Meridian." It does not appear on the annual reports in 1919 and 1920, but in 1920 it was moved as it was severely hampered at the original location by the ever moving sandbars in the river. Its installation, operation and maintenance at its new location, just east of the 4th Meridian, was borne jointly by both the Alberta and Saskatchewan governments. It has apparently been maintained in this way ever since, although it was moved again in 1925 to 25-53-28-5 and once or twice again to avoid sandbars.

Very often people coming down to the river to cross never knew which crossing would be in use. However, sometime in the 1960s, a 350-foot grade was built of stone, clay and gravel to make the crossing narrower, the resulting swifter current keeping the river free of sandbars. However, the ferry was again inoperative in 1974 for about ten days because of a sand bar which had built up during a low water period — showing, once again, that man will never be able to tame nature! Also, the faster current proved to be too much for the old wooden ferry and a new steel one had to be built.

130

Always a busy crossing, the ferry has carried foot passengers, loose animals, saddle horses, automobiles, trucks and heavy vehicles. In 1974 it carried almost 26,000 vehicles and 1,600 loose animals. It was not listed in the Alberta annual reports after 1962, but is apparently still operated on a 50-50 basis with Saskatchewan.

The first ferryman was Fred Hallett who, with his wife, lived in a little two-roomed house on the north bank of the river where they kept open house for travellers. He is remembered as a good ferryman and very kindhearted. One lady recalled that he used to row across the river to pick her up with her bread dough and take her across to bake it in the Hallett's oven.

A more recent ferryman, Peter Postnikoff, tells of a badger which was swimming across the river and in danger of being pulled underneath the ferry. He grabbed it by the back of the neck and threw it on to the ferry deck . . . where it bared its teeth and spat at him before disembarking.

MILK RIVER FERRIES
(1908)
Milk River

The only known "ferry" on the Milk River was a "sort of boat" constructed by a Mr. Satterlee in 1908, which he used to ferry people across when the railroad bridge at Milk River town was washed out. A Mr. Fitzmaurice used a four-horse team and wagon to ford the river with settlers and their effects, probably in the same year.

One unofficial way of crossing was by using the water surveyors' cable cars. A photograph shows Mounted Policeman A. Hamilton demonstrating this type of crossing on the Milk River near Pend d'Oreille. In later years Mr. Hamilton recalled that they used these cable cars by pulling on the cable between pulleys, hand over hand, if the cable car happened to be on the traveller's side of the river.

MIRROR LANDING FERRY
(1918-46)
Athabasca River

The Landing was a busy, important little place in the days when steamboats sailed along the Athabasca River — a jumping off place for traders, trappers and travellers, and early settlers on their way to the Peace River country.

The government ferry, installed as "Mirror Landing" in 1918, and so listed until 1923 when it changed to "Smith," was still kept busy while the north country was being settled. Traffic flow in the late 1920s necessitated a change to a Class A ferry, with two ferrymen. Winter crossings were made on the ice when it was firm enough, but settlers to the north were isolated in the spring and fall.

A local man built a small ferry of his own which he used after the government ferry was berthed for the winter. It was strong enough to plow through the thin ice but could carry only one truck at a time. The charge was $10 for a crossing, plus $1.00 per passenger, an exorbitant fee even today, but more so during the Depression years. However, the farmers were obliged to pay this fee to get across, not knowing when the ice would be strong enough. In case they objected and decided to wait, this local entrepreneur also maintained a few cabins and a store nearby, so travellers were forced to pay, one way or another. There were many complaints, Bill Katherens recalled, "until the government took over." Oldtimers recall a sad incident when a farmer and his family, moving from Saskatchewan to Fort St. John, all their possessions piled in a Chev car trailer, came down the river hill too fast. Not realizing that the river was at the bottom and not having brakes good enough to hold the heavily laden vehicle, the man plowed into the roadside bank to avoid running into the river. The whole outfit was wrecked and the man's wife and two of his children were killed outright. The farmer went on his sad, lonely way after his wife and the two children had been buried.

MITFORD FERRY
(1880s-1890s)
Bow River

In the early 1880s, the Hon. Thomas Cochrane and his wife, Lady Adela, daughter of the Earl of Stradbroke, chose a site for their home and their lumber and saw mills at the confluence of the Bow River and Horse Creek, just west of present-day Cochrane. They called their little settlement Mitford, after Mrs. Percy Mitford, a sister of Lord Egerton of Tatton in England. By 1885 there was, in addition to the Cochrane's "stately home," an hotel, a church, a store, livery stable and school, as well as Cochrane's mills. The Cochranes entertained many distinguished members of English nobility in their home.

A ferry was located at Mitford, under license of the North-West Territorial Government, probably in the vicinity of the railway bridge west of Cochrane. The NWMP annual report of 1888 noted the existence of ". . . a ferry at Cochrane near the coal mines. It shortens the distance between Calgary and Morley." It was also mentioned in the NWMP annual reports of 1890 and 1891, and was listed in the reports of the North-West Territorial Government. Because of difficulties caused by the impractical location of Mitford — a shortage of timber for the mills being the main drawback — the little settlement lasted only a few years. The Cochranes returned to England in 1898, giving up their dreams of an industrial empire.

MONARCH FERRY
1909
Oldman River

The annual report for 1909 states that the government installed a ferry on "the Oldman River west of Monarch." There is no further mention of this in any subsequent annual reports so the ferry may have been used by railway crews during that year only. The total cost for operation, materials and labour was only $523.31, so it was probably a small ferry, operated by the passengers themselves.

MORLEY FERRY
(1889-90-91)
Bow River

The 1889 annual report of the North-West Territorial Government indicates that it made "a grant of $75 to aid establishing a ferry on the Bow River at Morley." The ferry is mentioned in the North-West Mounted Police reports for 1890 and 1891. The 1893 report states that "good bridges have been built" and does not mention this ferry again.

MORRIN FERRY
(1913-59)
Red Deer River   SW15-31-21-4

Early settlers in this area either had to ford the river in summer or, after Fred Clegg arrived about 1909, travel across in his small rowboat "ferry" at what was known locally as "Clegg's Crossing." Fred, who ran a livery barn, also raised pigs on his homestead and carried many early settlers across the river before the government ferry was installed in 1913. He was the first government ferryman and when the site was being prepared, local residents helped to build the road down to the crossing west of Morrin. From that place, the ferry gave good service for forty-six years. It had to be taken out several times when the river was either too high or too low for it to operate but there were never any real difficulties. One incident occurred in 1938 when a large tractor proved to be too heavy and both ferry and tractor sank.

Residents wanted a bridge and sent an unsuccessful delegation to Edmonton in 1930 to ask for one. The ferry continued its operation until, in 1956, another delegation made a plea for a bridge. This time they succeeded, so the span was finally built and completed in 1959.

During the lifetime of the ferry, there is no record of the method of spring and fall river crossings, but winter crossings could usually be made on the ice. Mrs. Gladys Smith recalled an early spring day about 1924 when the wheels of their car broke through the ice and she and her baby sat in the car while her husband got the ferryman with a team of horses to pull them out.

Another early pioneer, Norman D. Stewart, recalled the day he and his brother were driving with team and democrat from Chinook to Didsbury. The Morrin ferry had been taken out for the winter and the river was covered with glare ice, with water flowing along underneath. To get to the nearest bridge would have entailed a seventy-mile journey of three or four days, just to get across the river. Their horses were not shod and if they both slipped on the ice it would probably have broken and they would all have gone under. Fortunately, the Stewarts were carrying four sacks of oats for the horses, so they emptied these into the democrat and tied the empty sacks on the feet of one horse and led him carefully across the thin, slippery ice, tethering him on the other side. They repeated the procedure with the second horse, hauled the democrat across, and were on their way.

MOUNTAIN HOUSE FERRY
(1916-17)
Red Deer River   NW8-35-3-5

Mountain House was a post office west of Innisfail during the early 1900s. The Raven bridge was built in 1911 so that farmers west of the river could cross to the railheads but in 1915 it was washed out and the government installed a ferry, which operated for two years until the bridge was rebuilt. The ferry operated at two locations; the second year it was moved downriver quarter of a mile, no doubt to also serve the bridge crew.

The name of the post office was changed to Moose Mountain shortly afterwards as it was too often confused with Rocky Mountain House.

MYRNAM FERRY
(1914-?, 1940s-1970)
North Saskatchewan River   NW18-55-8-4, N13-55-9-4

The village of Myrnam was incorporated in 1908 and the ferry was installed in 1914. It was listed as being "North of Mannville" by which name it appeared in the annual reports until 1927, changing to "N. of Myrnam" in 1928. This ferry enabled farmers and settlers north of the river to get across to Myrnam to sell their grain and get supplies, attend social events, doctors, and schools. Prior to 1914, they had to either ford the river or make the long journey around by the Brosseau ferry. A "cage" was installed on the ferry cable for spring and fall crossings, although some intrepid souls were known to have crossed in a rowboat, dodging large chunks of ice flowing down. Winter crossings were made on the ice when it was strong enough to carry vehicles. Foot passengers in winter had to depend on transportation awaiting them on the other side for the trip south to Myrnam. School children had to seek accommodation in Myrnam when the river conditions precluded the use of vehicles. One man did try an early crossing on the ice with a three-ton truck loaded with four tons of coal and sank in about ten feet of water.

Peter Bartoshyk also made a memorable trip across the river one spring, sitting in a looped rope on the high cable. He also recalled taking about eighteen head of cattle on the ferry from their pasture across the river. They decided to jump off the ferry in midstream but fortunately they all were able to swim to shore.

The Myrnam ferry was reclassified in 1938 as a Class A type, with two, three or four ferrymen operating in shifts, until the Myrnam bridge was opened to traffic in 1970. The last ride on the old ferry was made with many local dignitaries on board, including Mrs. Nick Bodnar, wife of its first ferryman of 1914, all in four vintage cars escorted by the local RCMP.

OLIVER FERRY
(1916)
North Saskatchewan River

A ferry was in operation at Oliver in 1916 only, although not listed in any government reports. Oliver, at that time, was a CNR flag station just outside of Edmonton; possibly the ferry was used by railway, bridge or construction crews during the year.

PANCRAS FERRY
(1916-24)
Red Deer River   14-22-4-4

Although this ferry was installed as "N. of Pancras," which was a CPR station at 21-4-4 (probably named after St. Pancras Station in London, England), the name had actually been changed to Cavendish by 1917. Cavendish was the name of the Duke of Devonshire, Governor-General of Canada from 1916 to 1921. The ferry was listed as "N. of Pancras" until 1923, changing to "Cavendish" in 1924. It is not listed in the annual reports after that year.

D. C. Cranston and his outfit cross the river at Peace River Crossing en route to Grande Prairie in 1909.

About 1920 or 1921, several ladies wanted to cross on the ferry from the south bank to attend a picnic on the north side. Three of them were rather large so Alec La Tromboise, the ferryman, put them all in a boat, thinking that it would be easier to take them across that way rather than take the ferry over. However, about fifty feet from shore the little boat sank and the ladies and Alec landed on a rock where they remained for about an hour until they were rescued. Some of the ladies already at the picnic site on the north bank were angry and said that Alec "should be hung." As they were handling a rope to help with the rescue, Alec's wife thought that they really were going to hang him so she delayed the rescue attempts by trying to get the rope away from them.

PEACE RIVER CROSSING FERRY
(1908-21)
Peace River

The history of this crossing goes back to the days of the early explorers and fur traders. Alexander Mackenzie wintered near the crossing in 1792-93 on his overland journey to the Pacific; many goldseekers passed this way on their way to the Klondike in 1898; and river boats sailed along the Peace River down to Vermilion Chutes, 325 miles from the crossing. The first settlers arrived about 1878; by 1905 the area was fairly well settled and a ferry was necessary for river crossing. The government built and installed a ferry in 1908 and it

136

carried many travellers during its thirteen years' of service until the bridge was built in 1922. Howard McRae (1978) told the story of the ferry at Peace River Crossing, where he arrived with his mother in 1914:

> I would have been about 7 years old . . . . I recall sitting on the beach watching the teams and wagons loading and unloading on and off this amazing conveyance [the ferry]. Many of the horses were getting on a ferry for the first time and their fright was understandable . . . the ferry had two large pontoons, pointed at each end, a traffic platform with rails, and attached to the platform were loading ramps at each end. Docking was always a frenzy of activity on the part of the ferryman, making sure the ferry ramp and the shore ramp met without a gap, getting passengers and teams ashore.

> A gas motor was eventually installed on the ferry, on a turntable between the two pontoons. About 1917-18, Model T Fords, Model 490 Chevs and a few Baby Grand McLaughlins started to arrive at the ferry crossing, causing great consternation amongst the horse population, whose inclination was to vacate the scene altogether. I can only recall two incidents at the ferry, one a fatality when a car drove down the hill on the east side of the river. The driver must have panicked, or missed his brake pedal, as he crashed through the restraining cable and was drowned. The other incident was when the ferry cable broke, the ferry floating downriver with its load and finally grounding a few miles downstream. In the spring and fall, a wagon box was attached to the trolley . . . to be wound across by hand.

> Early spring was the time for repair and maintenance of the ferry, a new coat of tar on the hull, in preparation for launching when the ice had gone. One spring launching was a little late as a severe winter had piled the ice 15 ft high above the river bank, partially covering the ferry, which had to be shovelled out.

On completion of the bridge, the ferry was finally retired, but the towers remained on the river banks, complete with the cable, for many years.

POCAHONTAS FERRY
(ca. 1910)
Athabasca River

A photograph captioned "Ferry on the Athabasca — above Pocahontas — ca 1910" was donated to Glenbow Museum. This places the ferry between Pocahontas and Jasper.

Pocahontas came to life about 1909 when the GTP railroad was being built and about fifty construction camps were set up in the area. Foley, Welch & Stewart were opening a tote road between Wolf Creek and Tete Jaune Cache about this time, so the ferry "above Pocahontas" may have been one of theirs, similar to the ferry they built and operated at Wolf Creek.

Pocahontas flourished from 1910 for about ten years, due to the fine seam of coal found there, which gave up almost a million tons of steam coal during the period. When this petered out, the little town of Pocahontas became a ghost town.

Pocahontas ferry, above, was probably used during the construction of the Grand Trunk Pacific in the Jasper area.

PURPLE SPRINGS FERRY
(1910-22)
Oldman River   11/14-15-4

When a ferry was moved to Purple Springs from north of Taber in 1910, no ferryman was appointed, the ferry being operated by the public at their own convenience.

Traffic was light, being mostly farmers and local residents going across to the railway or stores. However, the ferry was often on the other side of the river from the would-be traveller, so a rowboat was supplied, the traveller crossing in the boat, bringing back the ferry to where his goods, grain or livestock were waiting, and then crossing again on the ferry.

The ferry was first located on the river between the Judson farm and Pete Engleman's homestead, and Pete acted as the ferryman on many occasions.

RED DEER FERRIES
(1883-93)
Red Deer River

The first census taken by the North-West Territorial Government in 1881 reported no residents in the Red Deer Crossing area at all, but in May of 1882 the *Edmonton Bulletin* reported that ". . . a number of people are leaving Edmonton to settle at the Bow River [Calgary] Trail crossing of the Red Deer River," and June 1883 saw about thirty residents in the area.

In May 1882, a man named H. Meyer left Edmonton, taking with him the materials to build a ferry at the Red Deer Crossing, but this, apparently, did not materialize. The crossing at that time, according to NWMP reports, was about six hundred feet wide but only about two feet deep, far from ideal conditions for a ferry crossing. In June 1883 another man, R. Logan, came down from Edmonton carrying freight for the Hudson's Bay Company, and a skiff for use as a ferry at the Red Deer Crossing. This plan apparently fell through also, as the *Edmonton Bulletin* reported later in 1883 that "two settlers have a shanty near the Crossing and plan to put in a bridge or a ferry next season." In 1884 a ferry was reported to be "sunning itself on the river bank" and of no use to travellers at all.

In 1884, Sage Bannerman arrived at the Crossing via Calgary where three of his brothers had settled, and was authorized by the North-West Territorial Government to operate a ferry at the Crossing. By mid-June of 1884, Bannerman had a ferry in place at a cost of $800. During the ensuing three weeks, the heaviest rainfall ever experienced caused the river to rise rapidly, bringing down large quantities of driftwood and debris. This caught on the ferry cable and despite the efforts of Bannerman and his assistant, the cable broke and sank to the bottom of the river, the ferry very nearly following it. After a great deal of hard work the ferry was repaired and put into service by the end of the week, by which time there were about 125 wagons, carts and light rigs on each side of the river waiting to be ferried across.

In 1885, Bannerman — "Admiral" Bannerman, as he was known locally — rebuilt his ferry which had been named "The Irish Washerwoman" and he proclaimed that he "would have the best ferry in the North West Territories." However, the 1885 Rebellion put a stop to his plan and in April 1885 a company of militia comprised of sixty scouts under the command of Major Sam Steele, arrived at the crossing to find that the ferry had been severely damaged by ice during the spring break-up. They managed to ford the river safely, but the second echelon of soldiers under the command of Major Perry arrived at the crossing only to find that the river was in flood, about 250 yards wide, with a current of about $5\frac{1}{2}$ miles per hour. Perry and his men, including Lieutenant Normandeau, built a strong raft to carry themselves and all their guns and equipment across, but the rope broke as they were nearing the opposite side and the raft with its load floated downriver, eventually landing under a thirty-foot high cutbank. To get back to the Crossing, they had to make a detour around a large swamp and cut a road through heavy wood, the men hauling the gun, gun-carriage, ammunition, wagons and carts along with great difficulty. Back at the

It was a good time to beat the ferryman when the river was low. Here, a car fords the low waters of the Bow River while the Riverbow ferry lies beached.

Crossing, Perry and his men constructed a "ferry," somewhat hampered by a dispute between the ferryman and the owner of the lumber. Finally, 4½ days after they arrived at the Crossing, everything was ferried across and they went on their way to Edmonton. Major Perry reported that "the construction of this ferry was of the utmost importance. It completed the line of communication between Calgary and Edmonton, and obviated any delay to the column following."

After this, the North-West Territorial Government recognized the need for a permanent ferry at the Crossing so another one was built and installed, still known as "The Irish Washerwoman." This remained in service until 1893 when a bridge was built, it being washed out in the spring of 1899 by high water and floods. A new bridge was ready by 1903, but there is no record of a ferry being used at the crossing during the period 1899-1903, so apparently crossing had to be made by fording.

REDCLIFF
(ca. 1920)
South Saskatchewan River   7-13-6-4

In 1920, Fred Odlin sent a letter to the government asking for a ferry at this point, where the river was about 1,200 feet across. He asked for a light scow to hold one team and two small bridges to cross coulees on either side of the river. Local people offered to build roads to the ferry, which would save farmers a fourteen-mile trip. Meanwhile, the

140

Ajax Coal Mine across the river from Redcliff used a rowboat as a ferry, taking about seventy men over twice daily. Instead of providing a regular ferry, the government granted the Ajax Company $1,200 to build a bridge, which they had to maintain themselves.

RIVERBOW FERRY
(1915-38)
Bow River   27/28-15-16-4

The post office settlement of Riverbow, the site of an old Indian battle as well as stone writings, was incorporated as a township in 1909, although Riverbow itself consisted solely of a post office on the south side of the river. Residents of the township were mainly scattered farmers, although there were a few buildings on the north bank at one time, including a small church, and a schoolhouse built of straw bales.

By 1915 the area had become populated enough that a ferry was provided for farmers to cross the river to the railway and the supply centre at Brooks. During its years of service, the ferry carried only a limited traffic flow, due to the poor condition of the roads and approaches at the crossing. Also, the river at this point was very often too shallow for the ferry to operate and teams often had to ford. During the spring run-off, however, the high water was sometimes a problem in the years before it was controlled by the Bearspaw Dam. During periods of high or low water, or when ice conditions made ferry operation impossible, a home-made box conveyance was slung on the ferry cable on pulleys. This was large enough to carry two people, or one person and the mail sack, in rather cramped conditions. The ferryman would then haul the box across by hand.

Early ferrymen, who also acted as postmasters, lived in the little post office building, the only building at the crossing. In 1928, William Levette took over as postmaster and ferryman and had his wooden house hauled across the prairie to adjoin the post office.

The Riverbow area was extremely dry and subject to big dust storms, and eventually everyone moved away because of this. The ferry was discontinued in 1938, but the Bowslope (Scandia) ferry was only about eight miles away and the Bow City bridge was built in 1920.

ROCKY BUTTES FERRY
(1910-40)
Bow River   14/23-19-18-4

Installed as "S. of Bassano," the name of this ferry was changed to Rocky Buttes in 1912, and was listed in the annual reports by this name

A buggy carefully mounts the ferry at Rocky Mountain House in preparation for crossing the North Saskatchewan River.

until 1923. It changed to "Bredin's Crossing" in 1924, by which name it was listed until it was discontinued in 1941. It was also referred to locally as "Walsh's Ferry," as the crossing was on Redmond Walsh's land.

Local history tells of a training plane from the Claresholm airfield crashing into the ferry cable, wrecking the plane and causing some loss of life.

ROCKY MOUNTAIN HOUSE FERRY
(1908-46)
North Saskatchewan River   NE21-39-7-5

The old North West Company's fur trading post of Rocky Mountain House and the Hudson's Bay Company's post of Acton House, both built in 1799, were opened and closed several times for various reasons until their merger in 1821. The post then remained open periodically until 1876, when it closed for the last time.

At the turn of the century, incoming settlers were attracted by the agricultural possibilities of the district and the little settlement of Prairie Grange was established by the river ford, the post office being incorporated in 1908. It was always known by its old name of Rocky Mountain House, however, and the town was officially incorporated under this name in 1912.

By 1908 the population had increased to the extent that a ferry was necessary for river crossing, and one was to be built and installed in 1908. The government brought in all the materials necessary to build a ferry but they left the timber on the north bank of the river and the remaining material on the south bank. Hudson Hunt and Burl Gray, who were engaged to build the ferry, made a raft to bring the timber across to the south bank but high water swept the raft and all the timber about two miles downstream before it was stopped on a sand bar. They tied the raft to a tree but it got away again and that was the last they saw of both raft and timber.

Hunt and Gray returned to the settlement and, using a whipsaw, in three weeks they managed to hand saw enough timber for the ferry. When it was built and the cable stretched across the river, Hunt, Gray and young Wilfred Gray elected to ride across on the ferry's first trip, but once again, the river showed them who was the boss! The force of the current turned the ferry broadside and to avoid an accident they had to cut the rope holding the ferry to the cable, and the whole thing went off down river, where it was stopped by the same sand bar which had caught their raft. To haul the ferry back to the crossing entailed cutting a trail along the river bank for the team while the ferry was pushed out from the bank by men with long poles. When they finally got it in operation, two teams and wagons were lost when the frightened horses backed off the ferry into the river.

A railway bridge was built across the river in 1913 and although crossings on it were not officially permitted because of its open plank deck, supplies were hauled across on it during the spring and fall when the ferry was unable to operate. There is no record of any type of "cage" or box for winter crossings; instead, people apparently travelled on the ice. In later years, automobiles made illegal runs across the railway bridge, usually under cover of darkness which added to the danger. Many sick people were also carried over the bridge on stretchers on their way to the Red Deer Hospital.

The ferry carried many loads during its years of service — teams and wagons, cars, trucks, loads of lumber, gravel and steel, herds of horses, even small loads such as two small boys going for a swim in Crimson Lake. It also was used by the crews who built the traffic bridge in 1945 and was discontinued when the bridge opened to traffic a year later.

Burl Gray, who helped to build the first ferry, was the first ferryman, followed by O. E. ("Opie") Thompson, a kindly and popular man who ran it for twenty-five years.

ROLLING HILLS FERRY
(1954-74)
Bow River   NE36-13-13-4

In the early 1950s, the PFRA carried out a resettlement project,

The Rosevear ferry, near Peers on the McLeod River, is one of the few still operating in Alberta. It was started in 1914.

bringing about 180 families from flooded areas of Manitoba and Saskatchewan to the area south of Rolling Hills, where a similar project had been carried out during the dry years of the 1930s. The new settlement was named Hays, after David Hays, a manager of the former Canadian Land & Irrigation Company.

The government installed a ferry in 1954 as "S. of Rolling Hills" and this is listed in the annual reports until 1974. It apparently carried a lot of traffic as it was designated as a Class A ferry, with two ferrymen. A new bridge was built on Highway 875 and opened to traffic in 1975.

ROSEDALE FERRY
(1918-48)
Red Deer River

Rosedale came into existence about 1912 as a coal camp across the river from the Rosedale mine. At first, the river had to be crossed by walking along the ties of the railway bridge. A ferry was put into operation in 1918 and was kept fairly busy while the Star and Rosedale mines continued to operate. It was classified as a Class A ferry in 1929, with two, sometimes three, ferrymen operating it in shifts. It remained in operation until 1948 when the railway bridge was apparently converted for limited traffic use. The mines closed down in the early 1950s and Rosedale became a suburb of Drumheller with its swinging bridge, built in 1930, as a tourist attraction.

ROSEVEAR FERRY
(1914-present)
McLeod River   NW28-54-15-5

This ferry, north of Rosevear station, was installed for the benefit of settlers north of the river so that they could cross to the railhead and also to accommodate trucks belonging to companies carrying out logging operations north of the river. Harry Hellekson, who lived in the Thornton area, recalled the building of the first Rosevear ferry and waiting for the ferry crew to arrive. They arrived with two wagons, one the cook tent and camp outfit, the other all the tools and equipment.

The Thornton ferry, a few miles south-west, was also in operation for the first few years until the station there was closed, about 1920. Rosevear continued as a busy crossing, with heavy traffic and many foot passengers; according to records, it was carrying 600 to 800 pedestrians a month in 1929.

It has operated for about seventy years, apparently with no accidents or complaints about the service. It was reclassified as a Class A ferry in 1958, with two, sometimes three, ferrymen, continuing to carry a lot of traffic and heavy trucks. When the Alberta government decided, in 1971, to discontinue the ferry, along with other ferries throughout the province, people who were likely to be affected by the closure of the Rosevear ferry were invited to write to the government. They apparently did, as the Rosevear ferry remains in operation to the present time.

A long-time ferryman, Mike Iwanciwski, remained on the job twenty-one years, from 1953 to 1974.

ST. PAUL FERRY
(1901-07)
North Saskatchewan River

In 1901 the North-West Territorial Government granted a licence for the operation of a ferry at "St. Paul des Metis." However, as St. Paul des Metis (now St. Paul) was about fifteen miles away from the river, it is assumed that they meant the old St. Paul des Cris site (1865-1873) where the village of Brosseau is now located.

There were a number of early settlers in the old St. Paul des Cris district at the turn of the century and they soon required a means of crossing the river to get their grain to market. There is no record of the ferryman to whom the 1901 licence was granted, but local history records that Mathias Lambert operated a ferry there in 1904. This was the year Edmond Brosseau arrived on the area and started the little settlement which was to become Brosseau. Apparently Lambert's ferry operated until 1907 when the provincial government built and installed its own ferry *(see Brosseau Ferry)*.

SANDY LAKE FERRY
(1914-17, 1921-29)
35-55-1-5

Although it was not listed in its annual reports, the government installed a ferry on the narrows of Sandy Lake in 1914 to shorten the distance settlers had to travel to Morinville and Edmonton. Like other lake ferries with no current to carry it across, it was attached to a main cable which ran over a drum and crank which travellers had to turn to pull themselves across. Local residents who had used this ferry said that it was too small, that the cable drum was "homemade," and that it had no pump for pumping water out of the space under its deck. This is probably why it ended up floating around the lake, waterlogged and discarded, some time after 1917. That it was still in use in 1917 is confirmed by an early resident who recalled attending a corn feed at the narrows in that year.

In 1919 a group of local residents, including early settler, Ed Flynn, held a meeting to discuss the installation of a new ferry. After some controversy as to whether to build stone or wooden approaches, they eventually built wooden ones ready for the new ferry which was built at the site and put in operation in 1921. It was listed in the annual reports until 1929.

The amount of traffic was so small that no regular ferryman was appointed, the ferry with two sixteen-foot rowboats being operated by the public at their own convenience. The local rule, generally known to all, was that anyone using the ferry or one of the boats was to leave a craft on each side of the river. This usually worked quite well but once in a while both boats and the ferry would all be left on the same side of the river. This meant that the would-be traveller had to shout for Ed Flynn to turn out to get them across.

A causeway was built across the narrows in 1929 and the ferry ceased operation. On a skating trip around the lake in 1931, Gerald Heffernan, grandson of Ed Flynn found both the ferries beached on the Indian reserve, where their timbers probably remain to this day.

Gerald also recalled taking his horse and buggy across the narrows in 1921. The ferry was still running, but as he thought that the channel might freeze before his return trip, he took his horse across on the ferry and he and his brother, Dave, hauled the buggy across on ice which had formed on each side of the ferry channel.

Gerald's mother had a narrow escape on the ferry in 1929 when the cable broke halfway across the narrows. They envisaged being swept around the lake by the high wind and strong waves, but the cable jammed in the drum and Grandpa Flynn rescued them in his boat.

146

SANGUDO FERRY

(1909-50)

Pembina River   26-56-7-5

Before 1909, early settlers had to ford the river at this crossing, and in spring and fall, when the ice was melting or forming, the only way to cross was on the high railway bridge. This was a dangerous undertaking as the railway ties were spaced far enough apart that a person could fall through. Children were obliged to cross this way to attend school until the government installed a ferry in 1909. Frank Wright, one of the early settlers in the area, was the first ferryman as the McLeod Trail from Edmonton to Whitecourt crossed his land. Many early pioneers used the ferry on their way to their new homes and as Frank was not paid a salary, he was apparently allowed to charge tolls — five cents per foot passenger, fifteen cents for a horse and rider, and twenty-five cents for a team and wagon.

The ferry was listed in the annual reports for seven years by its land location only, then as "Wright's Crossing" from 1916 to 1937, and in 1938 it changed to Sangudo, the name of the settlement since the post office was first established in 1912. When the ferry was first put in, it was used by the Indians on their way to the Whitecourt trading post. They were fascinated by this novel way of crossing a river and would crowd on to the little ferry until it was jammed from end to end. Those who were unable to get on board would ford on horseback, trailing their pack ponies, and wait in a crowd on the opposite side to watch the intricacies of landing. The ferry also appears to have been used for religious services as a note in the local history recalls that about 1921 "Mr. Kuhn came to the ferry and baptized twelve children and four adults."

Although Frank Wright also opened his home as a stopping place for travellers, most whom enjoyed his homemade bread, pastries and sauerkraut, his son recalled that he was sometimes quite ill-tempered and "cranky as an old cougar." This gave him the name "Cougar" Wright, by which he is remembered by oldtimers. In the mid-1920s, Frank relinquished his job as ferryman in favour of Dave Lowry, his son-in-law, who continued in the job until 1936. No doubt an efficient ferryman, Dave was remembered for the night when the cowbell, which was used to call the ferryman to duty, sounded wildly. Dave rushed down to the crossing still in his nightshirt, thinking that it was just one of the bachelors, and he was halfway across the river, his nightshirt flapping in the wind, when the neighbour said, "You know, Dave, my wife is in the car." Dave was so embarrassed, he jumped into the river!

Dave's son, Clinton, who also helped to operate the ferry, recalled the time a couple of bank officials drove down the approach to the ferry crossing. The ferry had been taken out for the winter and there was about five inches of glare ice in the channel, covered with about two inches of water. The open touring car hit the ice and started to spin, with a stream of icy water spurting up on to the two men. The car didn't stop spinning until it ended up just short of the rapids, about two hundred yards downriver, and the two men walked back carefully on the watery ice.

There were the two other fellows who drove down and onto the ferry, and right off the other end. The car hung over the ferry apron and had to be hauled off after the two men, now sober, wet and cold, had been rescued from the icy water. The car, incidentally, a Gray Dort, remained on the river bank for many months; cars never got stripped in those days.

Local history records that the ferry crossing was moved about five miles downriver about 1937, although the annual reports make no mention of this. The ferry apparently discontinued in 1951 as a bridge had been opened to traffic just north of Sangudo.

SAWRIDGE FERRY
(1911-15)
Lesser Slave River

The Sawridge ferry was the only one recorded on the Lesser Slave River and was doubtless used by many travellers and early settlers on the old Athabasca Trail from Edmonton to Peace River. The settlement of Sawridge was quite large, with a population of 150 in 1911 and 500 in 1914. Many of the residents were listed as "ship's captains" who sailed the length of Lesser Slave Lake carrying settlers and cargo. A bridge was built at Sawridge about 1914, which was also about the time that the railway reached the settlement. Its name was changed to Slave Lake in 1922. During the floods of 1936, a ferry operated again at Slave Lake although it did not appear to be a cable-operated ferry and was probably only used during the flood season that year.

SHAFTESBURY FERRY
(1977-present)
Peace River

As early as 1917, local farmers who wanted to get across the river to and from market with their produce and supplies, petitioned the government for a ferry at this point. However, the petition was turned down, as the Peace River Crossing ferry was only eight miles downriver. Sixty years later the government installed a ferry to take the

place of the privately-owned and operated Blakeley Ferry *(see refer-*
ence) which had operated for about twenty-six years. After consider-
ing suggestions from local residents, the name Shaftesbury was
chosen for the new ferry crossing, in view of its long and historical
association in the area, and on 17 June 1977, the Hon. Dr. H. M.
Horner, Deputy Premier and Minister of Transportation, cut a ribbon
to officially inaugurate the new Shaftesbury Ferry service.

SHANDRO FERRY
(1906-62)
North Saskatchewan River   NW34-57-15-4

Many families, including the Shandros, came to western Canada
from Bukovina (now the Ukraine) under the Laurier immigration plan.
They settled on both sides of the river around the turn of the century,
and the only means of crossing at this point was in a rowboat operated
by Maria Solowan, daughter of settlers on the north bank. She
charged a crossing fee of five cents.

In the spring of 1906, Andrew Shandro (later to be the first Member
of Parliament of Ukrainian descent) organized local residents into
work parties to cut out the steep approaches to the crossing. Meanwhile, a government ferry was built in Edmonton and floated down to
Shandro where Nicolai Moisey was appointed ferryman. He lived in a
small shack on the north bank. The ferry was kept busy with more and
more settlers arriving in the area, as well as travellers, mailmen, the
Mounted Police, salesmen and agents. It remained in operation with
one ferryman until it was reclassified as Class A in 1930, when two,
sometimes three, ferrymen worked in shifts. The Shandro ferry experienced all the vagaries of the river, especially in the spring run-off
period, when the river rose rapidly; it was quite common to see dead
animals, trees, and even small buildings, floating downstream. There
were no recorded accidents, except for ferryman Gordon Haines who
fell off the ferry in 1925 and was drowned, but there were many
anxious moments as winter travellers risked thin ice to cross.

Tom Shandro (Andrew's son) recalled that the worst flood on
record happened in 1914, which probably meant that the ferry could
not operate regularly through that season. However, a riverboat — a
waterwheel-propelled freighter — made its appearance in 1914, also in
1915 when flooding continued, commuting twice weekly from the
John Walter Flats in Edmonton and carrying supplies for settlers along
the river as far as Shandro. Next day it turned around and worked its
way back to Edmonton taking grain and livestock.

It may have been during one of these years when the Victoria
(Pakan) ferry escaped and floated downriver with a full load. The

Named after its first operator, Steven Hall, the Steveville ferry was a longtime landmark on the Red Deer River.

Shandro ferryman, advised of the runaway and with the help of local residents tied strong ropes and cables across the river on trees on each bank to catch the runaway, but just as it was caught on these, they, too, snapped and the ferry travelled several miles further along before it was finally caught and anchored to a huge tree. The terrified people on board were taken to Andrew Shandro's home to recover from their six-hour trip down the raging, rampaging river.

STEERFORD FERRY
(1901-22)
Red Deer River

The North-West Territorial Government, in its 1900 annual report, stated that it "partly completed the work of providing a ferry across the river at Prince's Crossing, north of Medicine Hat." The next year it stated that "the ferry was completed at Steerford." The ford at this location was on the old trail from Medicine Hat to Battleford, used by many early travellers and the Mounted Police. It was also used by many early ranchers to cross their cattle herds, hence the name "Steerford." The ferry was known by many names — Steerford, Prince's Ranch, Prince's Crossing, Fitger's ferry, and even "North of Bindloss." The crossing was originally on land owned by Hector Prince, who was drowned while helping to take cattle across the river. His ranch was eventually bought by Eugene Fitger who ran a rooming house and operated the ferry for several years.

The ferry was damaged by floods in 1916 so the government built a new scow and re-installed it as "North of Bindloss" in 1917, after which it was listed once again in the annual reports as Prince's Ranch until it was discontinued in 1922 when a bridge was built near the crossing. The ferry approaches were kept in good repair by farmers and settlers who organized "work bees" to do the job, so that they could get into Bindloss to sell their grain and get supplies.

Winter crossings were made on the ice, but in spring and fall, without the benefit of a "cage" on the cable, some hardy souls would climb the cable towers, put a pulley on the cable with a looped rope attached to sit in and push themselves off. This would get them to the half-way point, when they had to pull themselves over the rest of the way.

Harry England was remembered as a ferryman who rescued six people whose car went off the end of the ferry into deep water. It is reputedly at this crossing, too, that two ladies were drowned when crossing with their team and democrat.

STEVEVILLE FERRY
(1910-70)

Red Deer River   4-22-12-4, NW4-22-12-4, NE33-21-12-4

Steven Hall and his wife started their homestead by the river in 1909. They also built a store, a boarding house and a livery barn and, when the ferry was installed in 1910 Steve also acted as ferryman. The area, formerly Cravath Corners, quickly became known as Steveville, after the hospitable and hardworking Hall. He ran the ferry for two years, then, in 1912, one of his employees, Ambrose Shaw, was appointed and continued as the ferryman until 1928. As one pioneer commented.:

> I came to Alberta from Ontario in 1910, when I was 20. I headed east across the prairie towards the Steveville ferry. It was not working so I crossed the river on an ice jam . . . stopped at Steve Hall's . . . Steve and his wife were wonderful people with hearts of gold . . . Steve had a pile of dinosaur bones on the ferry landing . . . the hill from the river was so steep they had to carry loads up by hand as horses couldn't manage the weight. (Norman D. Stewart, 1980).

Another oldtimer remembered Ambrose Shaw:

> In 1913 . . . we had to cross the Steveville ferry . . . the ferryman's name was Mr. Shaw. Whatever time of night you came to the ferry, he was always there to meet you.

The ferry appears to have had quite a busy time. In 1917, it took thirty-two loads of wheat across in one day. It was designated as a Class A ferry from 1938 to 1943 (two ferrymen), back to Class B (one ferryman) in 1946, and back to a Class A from 1947 until 1970.

When the Sunniebend bridge was washed out in 1935, the old reliable ferry was put back into service. Guiding the craft across the Pembina River (left to right) are Charlie and O. P. Adair.

The ferry was installed in 1910 at NW4-22-12-4, but another location, NE33-21-12-4 appears in another record. However, a bridge was built in 1970 on the first location, so the ferry may have been moved a short distance away.

SUMMERVIEW FERRY
(1904-17)
Oldman River   16-7-29-4

Early settlers had been obliged to ford the Oldman River at this point until the ferry which had been operating temporarily at Fort Macleod was, according to the 1904 Annual Report of the North-West Territorial Government, "moved up river to a point near Pincher Creek, and was a source of relief to the settlers on the north side of the river." It was located about 1½ miles north of the highway, directly north of the Maunsell crossing, its maximum capacity being a four-horse team and wagon, plus a two-horse team with a democrat or buggy.

The ferry apparently operated on a toll system, even after 1905. According to an account book kept by William Glass, who operated it from 1910 to 1912, the toll charges ranged from 10 cents to 65 cents, probably depending on what the traveller was taking across. The government also paid a monthly "grant" to the ferryman ($60 in 1912) and it is assumed that the ferryman also kept the toll charges. William Glass died in 1912, so this may have been the last year that the ferry operated under a toll system.

On the road to the ferry from the south there were two gates on the Liddell farm and the story goes that Liddell cut a hole in the wall of his house so that he could watch to see that both gates were closed by ferry users as they passed through.

The ferry often broke loose, usually in the spring flood waters, but local residents always helped to haul it back to the crossing. Charles LaFrance was the ferryman in 1915 when the river flooded and he had to rescue his wife from their small house on the south bank. He also managed to rescue a newborn colt from the river near the ferry after it had fallen from a cutbank. On another occasion a herd of cattle loaded on to the ferry caused it to tip on edge, all the animals sliding off into the river, and in 1917 the ferry broke loose and floated about a mile downriver with several passengers and a car on deck.

The ferry was replaced by a bridge at about the same location in 1918, but when another bridge was built near Brocket in 1923, the small Summerview bridge was dismantled.

SUNNIEBEND FERRY
(1910-20, 1935-36)
Pembina River   10-61-7-4

The post office settlement of Sunniebend, established in 1910, saw its first settlers as early as 1906 when the Adair family took up homesteads on each side of the river. Before 1910, when the government installed a ferry on the Adair land, the river could be forded either at Adairs or further up river on Carl Antonsen's land. The post office was located at Adair's home and the ferry also was installed there. According to local history, it was operated by the public themselves during its first year. Two small rowboats were supplied, one for each side of the river, so that would-be ferry users could row across and bring it over when required. However, Charles Adair would sometimes act as the ferryman and his attention could be attracted by banging on an iron triangle which hung from the branch of a tree.

The Sunniebend post office was closed in 1916 after the railway was built east of the river and Pibroch became the mail centre. The problem of getting mail across Wabash Creek during flood periods was solved with ingenuity by Ernest Gamble of Pibroch, who trained his dog to swim the creek, towing a small raft carrying the mail, to be met on the other side by a Sunniebend resident. As the Sunniebend community grew, residents decided that the ferry was outdated and that a bridge was needed, so they cut and hauled the timber and built a small wooden structure in 1921, and the ferry was discontinued.

According to local history, this bridge was washed out in 1926, and the use of a ferry was again required. The annual report shows that a ferry was installed as "Antonsen's Crossing" which the public had to operate themselves as traffic was so light *(see Antonsen's Ferry).* A new steel bridge was planned and after some local controversy as to its location — Adairs or Antonsens — it was built at about the same place as the old wooden bridge at SW15-61-27-4 and opened for traffic in 1931.

However, this bridge was washed away in the 1935 spring break-up, when great chunks of ice roared down the turbulent river, and once again a ferry was installed using the old Sunniebend ferry landings, until the bridge was repaired.

TABER FERRY
(1906-10)
Oldman River

This ferry served as a river crossing for four years until the McLean bridge was built in 1910. The annual report for that year stated that

> on completion of a bridge over the Belly Oldman River at Taber, the ferry formerly operated at this point was moved down and operated north of Purple Springs.

TAYLOR FLATS FERRY
(1920s)
Peace River

Although this ferry was actually in British Columbia, it is included here because it was used by Albertans in the Cherry Point area who referred to it as the Cherry Point ferry.

Donald Herbert (Herbie) Taylor and Bob Barker, homesteaded side by side on the flats by the river. Taylor apparently arrived there first, in 1912, and his wife Charlotte, a Cree Indian, ran the post office and was also well experienced in the use of medicinal herbs.

In the early days, they crossed the river by rowboat or dug-out, but in the early 1920s a ferry was installed and Herbie took over as ferryman. He put up a large sign at the ferry landing proclaiming it to be "TAYLOR FLAT" but when he went off on his trapline, Barker would take Herbie's sign down and erect his own which designated the area as "BARKER'S FLAT." When Herbie returned, down would come the Barker sign and up would go the Taylor sign.

On one occasion, the small ferry loaded with cattle capsized throwing animals and passengers into the river, but they all managed to scramble to safety. Soon after this a motor-driven ferry was installed, which remained in use until the Alaska Highway was built. During spring and fall river conditions, passengers and mail were transported in boats if there was open water, or pulled across on sleighs when the ice was firm, both crossings being often quite dangerous.

At present-day Taylor, the Church of the Good Shepherd stands in memory of the four daughters of a Mr. Hofstrom who were all drowned in an accident at the ferry in August 1932.

THORNTON FERRY
(1912-20)
McLeod River   10-54-16-5

This ferry, installed in 1912, served the few homesteaders who had settled around the old Wolf Creek area when the railway bridges were being built for the Grand Trunk Pacific and Canadian Northern Railways. It provided access to the railhead for farmers north of the river.

Harry Hellekson, a former ferryman himself, said that his family moved to the Thornton district in 1917 so that the children could attend school. They lived close to the ferry and Harry recalls that a "basket" hanging from the ferry cable took passengers and their goods across the river during the spring and fall river conditions. In the spring of 1917, Harry helped the ferryman, Hank Tomlinson, to take quite a large amount of freight across in the basket, which also had seating capacity for four people. They had to haul it across by means of a short rope attached to a drum and buggy wheel.

TINDASTOLL FERRY
(1898)
Red Deer River

A ferry service for the Icelandic colony at Tindastoll (now Markerville) was started when the North-West Territorial Government instructed Dominion Land Surveyor Angus McPhee to install a ferry there for the settlers' use. The ferry was washed downriver by high water in May of 1899 and after being put back into service, it remained in operation until the early spring of 1901, when it was carried away again.

After that, a small boat was used to carry passengers only. A bridge was built in 1902, thus doing away with the ferry which (says the North-West Territorial Government report)

from the time of its establishment has been a considerable source of trouble and annoyance both to the Department and to the public.

The location of the ferry is not recorded, but a history of Innisfail indicates that it was in operation about 3½ miles north-west of the town, operated in the early 1900s by Frank Thomson who had arrived in the west from Quebec in 1883. Frank had worked for the Hudson's Bay Company at Rocky Mountain House for a while and had married Chief Poundmaker's daughter. Their son, Frank Thomson, interviewed in 1980, recalled the ferry in his boyhood days and his father's sorrel horse which used to swim across the river after the ferry.

TOLMAN FERRIES
(1907-25, 1946-64)
Red Deer River

In 1906 and 1907, when the area between Trochu and Rumsey was being settled, the railway was located west of the river, which meant that a ferry was necessary for farmers and settlers on the east side. In 1907, the government floated the old Content ferry downriver to a point designated as "East of Olds," the name by which it was officially listed until 1911. The name changed to "Trochu" from 1912 to 1916, when it was listed as the "Tolman" ferry, being located on land owned by the Tolman brothers. Oldtimers remember it also as the "Stonepile" ferry because of its proximity to a prehistoric stone monument on a nearby hilltop.

The ferry carried many new settlers and their effects, as well as mail and supplies during its early years. Ted Postill, who ran the ferry in 1908, recalled taking settlers across with all kinds of conveyances —wagons, carts, prairie schooners — and helping them with their goods and livestock. A carrier was attached to the cable to take mail and supplies across in the spring and fall, winter crossings were probably made on the ice. One early resident, according to local history, decided to cross on the overhead cable, hand over hand, with a rope around his waist attached to the cable for safety. When halfway across he lowered himself on his rope for a short rest and was unable to pull himself up to the cable again. He was discovered later in the day, exhausted and panic-stricken, dangling from the end of his rope, and was rescued with the use of the carrier which was kept on the west side of the river.

The old Tolman ferry service was discontinued in 1924 because of the light traffic and also because of the age of the scow, which had seen much service, first at Content, then at Tolman. By then a railway line had been built from Drumheller to Stettler so there was no longer the necessity for crossings from the east.

Petitions for re-establishment of the Tolman ferry were made in 1932, as there was a sixty-mile stretch of river with no crossings, the nearest points being the Content bridge and the Morrin ferry. After fourteen years of petitions from local residents of Trochu, the Chamber of Commerce, and the Municipal Districts of Starland and

Ghost Pine, a new ferry was finally built and installed in August of 1946. A three-room dwelling was also built for the ferryman. In spite of objections by the Tolman family, who did not want the ferry on their land, and petitions from other residents that the ferry crossing location be changed, it was installed at the same location as the old ferry, where it served for another eighteen years until the Trochu bridge was opened to traffic, on Highway S585, in 1964.

VICTORIA FERRY
(1892-1972)
North Saskatchewan River   NW 12-58-17-4

The old Victoria district with its rich soil, pasture, timber and a good climate, had been a meeting place for Indians and Metis for many years before the white man settled here. The Rev. Robert Rundle visited the area in the mid-1840s, and a Methodist mission was established there about 1862 by the Reverends George McDougall, Henry Steinhauer and Thomas Woolsey. A Hudson's Bay Company trading post was also built about the same time.

There is no record of a ferry being used during these early years, but after the arrival of the North-West Mounted Police in 1874 and with more settlers coming into the area, the need for a ferry became a matter of some importance.

Supt. A. H. Griesbach of the NWMP, Fort Saskatchewan noted in his 1888 Annual Report:

> There is only one point where the North Branch [of the Saskatchewan River] can be crossed at all conveniently. A cable ferry is required opposite this town to enable the northern country to be reached.

His 1889 and 1890 reports contained specific recommendations for a ferry at Victoria:

> A ferry at Victoria would be a great convenience, both to the general public and to the police, as the road from here to Victoria on the south side of the river, besides being better than the one on the north, having only three creeks to cross, one of which is well bridged, is considerably shorter. Freighters from Calgary could then proceed direct to Saddle Lake and the Lac la Biche district via Victoria, shortening the route considerably.

In the 1892 report, after five years of recommendations, Griesbach was able to state that there was

> a ferry at Victoria. The last named ferry has been put in this year and was strongly recommended by me in previous reports. It is a great convenience to settlers at Victoria and Egg Lake, and also to the travelling public.

The ferry remained in service, under license of the North-West Territorial Government, carrying travellers, freighters, settlers, police, Indians and missionaries, until it was taken over by the new province in 1905.

Frank Mitchell who arrived at Victoria with his parents in 1899 at the age of seven, recalled crossing on the old ferry, operated by Louis Thompson. According to Frank, the ferry had to be pushed upstream for half a mile and then rowed across, the current bringing it back to the landing. It is not clear whether this performance was necessary for every crossing or just in certain river conditions.

In 1906, the new provincial government's annual report noted that

> on account of the scow at Victoria being too small and not suitable to meet traffic requirements at that point, the old Clover Bar ferry was floated down and installed at Victoria.

The old ferry was taken upriver and installed north of Lamont, at the post settlement of Eldorena, just east of present-day Redwater.

The Pakan ferry, to which its name was changed in the 1909 annual report, saw many adventures during its further sixty-six years of service. On one occasion it was overloaded with lumber and had a dozen people on board when the cable broke and the ferry drifted downriver. The ferryman rowed to shore in the emergency rowboat and ran two miles to a phone to alert the Shandro ferryman further downriver where the Pakan ferry, with its load of frightened passengers, was rescued.

Winter crossings on the ice were usually successful but an elderly couple tried it one day when the ice was unstable. Their horse went through the ice, leaving their wagon sitting precariously on top, but all were resuced. On another occasion, two ladies managed the ice crossing with their team and buggy on a hurriedly constructed "bridge" of dead trees, planks and brush. The hind part of a Model T once went under with the engine still running, appearing to make an effort to scramble out.

Crossings in spring and fall were hazardous, but mail and supplies went across in either a rowboat pushed across the soft ice, or in a basket on the ferry cable.

VINCA FERRY
(1913-66)
North Saskatchewan River   SW36-56-21-4

Installed as "North of Bruderheim," little is known of this ferry. Vinca was a small farming settlement and post office about seven miles south of Redwater and although railways were available both north and south of the river, the Vinca and the Eldorena ferries were obviously necessary for over fifty years. The first ferryman at Vinca was William Puchalik. The first time he took his new car on the ferry it ran off the other end and his little daughter, Annie, fell into the river. Fortunately she was wearing a straw hat tied by ribbons underneath her chin and this kept her afloat until her father, in a rowboat, saved her about a mile downriver.

A later ferryman recalled one or two cases of drowning while he was ferryman but no details of these accidents are available. In later years, the Vinca ferry was used extensively by oil company employees until the Redwater bridge was built on Highway 38 in 1967.

WARSPITE FERRY
(1920-63)
North Saskatchewan River   SW19-59-18-4

Originally named "Frances Siding," then "Smoky Lake Centre," the village of Warspite came into being in 1916, apparently named after the British warship HMS Warspite. The ferry was installed in 1920 and operated until the Waskatenau bridge was opened to traffic in 1963. The Pakan and Waskatenau ferries also operated a few miles to the east and west.

Not much of the early history of the ferry is recorded, except that it was moved at some time to the above location from its original location about two miles upriver. Mike Melnyk, who was the ferryman for about twenty years from the mid-1940s, recalled the many passengers, some with teams and wagons, seemed to want to cross every half hour between midnight and 7:00 am. He had to be awake and dressed to take each one across for 25 cents per vehicle and five cents per passenger.

Mike said that the Warspite crossing had a much faster current than many other ferry crossings on the river. It was sometimes difficult to turn the ferry with a crank, so a pilot wheel was installed about 1951, giving more leverage to turn the craft into the current. A shelter was also built over the pilot wheel, affording protection for the ferryman when it rained. Prior to this, he just got soaked in a rainstorm. About 1954 a motor was installed, by which the ferry was pulled straight across the river by a cable on the down current side, making the ferryman's job much easier. There is no record of any serious accidents at the ferry, except the time a pickup truck hit Mike and knocked him into the river, tearing the ligaments in his foot.

WASKATENAU FERRY
(1921-63)

North Saskatchewan River   32/33-58-19-4

About 1920 or 1921, the farmers south of the river at this point formed the Waskatenau Ferry Board and built and operated their own ferry to get across to the railway. The first ferryman on this private ferry was Fred Henson, who also built a little log cabin at the crossing. The annual report of 1924 states that "the ferry was taken over from the Waskatenau Ferry board" in that year, and was listed in the 1925 annual report as a government ferry. It apparently used the private ferry for a few years until a new scow was built for the crossing in 1928.

Asher Warr was the ferryman for the first ten years (his wife, Mrs. Amy Warr later became Provincial President of the UFWA). Their daughter, Dorothy Shook of Edmonton recalled:

> Our farm joined the ferry road allowance . . . our house was about half a mile from the crossing so it took a lusty "Halloo" to get Dad on a horse and down to the river. The government built a ferry house in 1928 and Dad sold his farm and moved down to the river every summer while the ferry was in operation . . . . traffic in the early days was mostly horses and wagons. The hills on both sides of the river were very steep and early cars were not equal to the climb, and had to be pulled or pushed to the top. New approach roads were built in 1927, not quite so steep, but these were still the days of dirt roads and when it rained, it was still a problem to get up and down in the slick mud.
>
> The ferry was a popular place for social gatherings and people came from all around for corn roasts, potato roasts, singing, dancing and bonfires. The rough planks of the ferry deck were swept clean and we danced to the music of violin and mouthorgan on lovely summer evenings. Dad didn't drink, so no liquor was allowed. Mother was a good cook and there was always lots of food. People wanting to cross on the ferry were welcome to join the party.
>
> One summer there was a big fight — the ferry assistant had informed on two neighbours who were making moonshine and they came after him with a rifle. Shots were fired and horses turned loose so that pole pins and neck yokes could be used as weapons, but the ferry assistant wisely took the ferry over to the other side of the river.
>
> There was great excitement one day, about 1931, when famous bush pilot "Punch" Dickins made a forced landing near the ferry. My husband drove him to Edmonton for parts to repair his plane.
>
> I left the district in 1935.

The ferry continued in operation until 1963 when the Waskatenau bridge was opened to traffic.

WATINO FERRY
(1915, 1938-54)

Big Smoky River   10-78-24-5

Installed in 1915 for the convenience of incoming settlers as "West of McLennan," this ferry operated for that year only according to annual reports. The railway was being constructed at this point and a railway bridge was built. However, even though this was the only means of crossing the river, its use was forbidden to pedestrians. Many petitions were sent to the government asking for the ferry to be reinstated — from the UFA, from Father St. Pierre, the priest at Tangent, from the residents of Girouxville and "Pruden's Crossing" as it was known locally. The government engineer, A. H. McQuarrie, also recommended at a later date that a ferry be installed but when the government finally decided in 1939 to install a ferry, petitions were then signed for a bridge. Ferry service commenced in 1939, with many people petitioning for the job of ferryman.

Flood waters and driftwood broke the cable in 1943 and the ferry drifted away to a point about nine miles south of Peace River town. It was rescued by a government crew who had to obtain a power boat to help the ferry make the return journey back to Watino. The journey took 2½ days, travelling over sixteen rapids, through the driftwood and high waters.

It was designated as a Class A ferry, with two ferrymen, in 1944.

There was a tragic accident at the crossing in 1952 when two ladies, en route to a homecoming party in Spirit River, were thrown off the ferry and drowned when it tilted after the loading apron worked loose and the two cable towers collapsed.

Although the *Grande Prairie Herald* started to report the expected retirement of the Watino ferry in 1953, it was not until the summer of 1955 that the newspaper carried the following item:

"The Peace River country has said farewell to the ferry which has plied for so many years across the Smoky River at Watino. Completion of the bridge this spring meant that it was unnecessary to put the ferry into the water again."

WEMBLEY FERRY
(1930-ca. 1970)
Wapiti River   SE11-70-8-6

Known locally as the Pipestone Creek ferry, or "HMS Pipestone," this ferry was built and installed in 1930. District Engineer A. H. McQuarrie recalled in his memoirs that he always felt that not enough time was spent in selecting a location for this crossing and his feelings were borne out by the many mishaps which occurred to successive ferries here. However, when it was working, the ferry afforded a means of crossing for settlers south of the river to get to the railhead at Wembley. It carried many passengers — homesteaders, farmers, trappers, lumbermen, and oil crews — in its time. It also transported

Frigid temperatures marked the end of another season for the tireless ferries. Here, the Wembley ferry is ready to be pulled out for the winter in the late 1940s.

hundreds of people in the earlier years on berry-picking expeditions; in 1932, three to four hundred people used it on weekends for those important trips to obtain what was probably the only fruit available in the depression years.

The ferry made several unscheduled trips downriver, breaking away from its cable in floods and high water conditions in an effort to make its way to the Arctic. It also made an effort to get to the bottom of the river on a number of occasions, being waterlogged and swamped by high water, but "HMS Pipestone" was always caught or pumped dry again to continue in service.

There were a couple of years when it was able to continue in operation until just before Christmas, being hauled out just before the holiday but leaving several hunters and trappers stranded in the bush on the wrong side of the river.

In 1948, a small private ferry owned by the Ross Lumber Company had to be moved to the crossing when the "HMS Pipestone" broke loose and was carried down to the Grovedale ferry crossing, causing considerable inconvenience to cream shippers, hog raisers and to the local lumber mills which had several million feet of timber ready to cross. In 1949 the government installed an extra cable to enable the ferry to be hand-wound across, as the water was too low for regular crossings, and in 1951, in a bid to save the ferry from the ravages of the Wapiti River's uncertain moods, a gasoline motor was added. Cross-

162

ings in the winter were made on the ice if it was strong enough, but in the spring of 1952, an "aerial passenger carrier" was constructed to operate on the ferry cable. This consisted of a twelve-inch plank bolted to 2x4's, fixed on to two airplane wheels (salvaged from a wrecked plane found in the mountains). This formed a unique conveyance on which travellers sat and pulled themselves across, hand over hand, by the cable. It was used for many years and carried tons of mail and supplies across the river.

In 1953, the ferry remained in the river until late November, being pulled back and forth through the slush ice by a "cat," moving supplies and equipment across for lumber and oil companies.

A long-awaited bridge was finally opened to traffic in 1968, but pressure for continuation of the ferry from local farmers and hunters resulted in the formation of the Wembley Ferry Association which bought the ferry and equipment, including the two ferryman's houses, and operated "HMS Pipestone" on a toll basis. For a $10 membership in the Association, people could cross as often as they wished. This continued for two or three years for the benefit of farmers, hunters and travellers, but the venture was not a success and the old ferry was left to stagnate for several years before being restored and placed on display at Pipestone Creek Park, south of Wembley.

WHITECOURT FERRY
(1922-27)
Athabasca River   NW¼12-21-23-4

The provincial government, according to its 1922 annual report, "built and installed a new ferry at Whitecourt" and it was listed in its reports until 1927. Local history records, however, that the ferry was established privately by the Western Construction & Lumber Co. to transport men and supplies to lumber camps north of the river. This seems reasonable, as there were only two families settled north of the river at that time.

There is no record of a ferryman being appointed by the government in 1922, but one was on the job in the following year and a shack built by the crossing for his use. Again, it is not certain whether he was employed by the government or by the lumber company.

In 1927 the government engineer recommended that the ferry be discontinued and that perhaps the lumber company could keep it in operation. In that year, also, the government received a letter from an irate homesteader saying that the ferryman had refused to take him and his sick wife across the river to the doctor and had "threatened to shoot him." A raft had to be quickly built to take the sick lady across.

References to the ferry disappeared from the annual reports in 1927 but it was apparently still being run by the lumber company. A petition was received by the government in 1928 indicating that the two remaining settlers north of the river would be marooned and their children would not be able to attend school if the ferry was not maintained. It was also required by fire rangers and the Whitecourt Board of Trade wrote to the government in favour of it in 1930. It appears that the ferry was still being used by the lumber company but a report in 1931 indicated that it was in very poor condition. Another petition was sent to the government in 1931 by both settlers and the Board of Trade, but not until 1944 was the ferry rebuilt by the lumber company at its own expense. It can only be assumed that they continued to operate it themselves, for their own employees, and the the various petitions indicated, perhaps, that the ferry was not available for the general public.

WILD HORSE FERRY
(1909-15, 1913-22)
Pembina River   S24-57-5-5

Wild Horse was a small settlement but the surrounding area was fairly well settled by 1909, when Charlie O'Neill built a small private ferry on his land. It could carry only one team at a time and no heavy wagons could use it. The O'Neill ferry operated until 1915, when it was lost in the floods. The government had built and installed a ferry at S24-57-5-5, close to the range line in 1913, which remained on their annual reports until 1922.

In the absence of government records, and in view of local history which relates that the O'Neill ferry appears to have been salvaged and moved upriver to "Barny" Barnhouse's land, it is not clear how many ferries were operating in this area. Apparently the farmers downriver wanted the ferry to stay at O'Neill's, but farmers upriver went late one night to O'Neill's and took the ferry, cable and all, to the Barnhouse crossing, where it is reputed to have been operated by Barnhouse until the bridge was opened to traffic in 1923.

WOLF CREEK FERRY
(1910-12)
McLeod River

This, the first known ferry on the McLeod River, was a private one, built, owned and operated at the hamlet of Wolf Creek by railway contractors Foley, Welch & Stewart. This was the head of steel for both the Grand Trunk Pacific and Canadian Northern Railways as both lines were pushing west, only a few miles apart. Two railway bridges were built, one over Wolf Creek, the other over the McLeod River about half a mile west of the creek. The ferry was maintained not far from the bridges to transport their crews and materials across the river.

The construction crews about this time numbered about 2,000 men and the tiny hamlet of Wolf Creek developed into a rip-roaring little town. It had an hotel, a bank, several stores, a dozen restaurants, pool rooms, a drug store, barber shop, a couple of blacksmith shops, and a real estate office, not to mention the usual establishments which proliferated around construction camps — brothels, gambling dens and bootleggers' establishments. All railway crews were under a law of prohibition so there were no bars as such.

The little ferry served the crews and the few early settlers in the area until 1912, when Wolf Creek, never destined to become a permanent town, had become deserted. The Rev. J. Burgon Bickersteth, in his book, *The Land of Open Doors*, recalled that he had passed through the district about 1912 and found only a ghost town, the stores and barns deserted, most of them roofless and windowless. However, to serve the few homesteaders who had settled in the area, the provincial government built and installed a ferry in 1912 at roughly the same location, which was by that time known as Thornton.

V
Alberta Ferrymen

The following is a list of names of all Alberta's ferrymen which could be located. The lack of official documents for the period between 1905 and 1924, however, means that names of many early ferrymen are missing unless they have been recorded in local histories.

Allendale Ferry: George Ritchie (1914), Paul Linehan (1915-35), Lorne Gray (1936-39), S. Brown (1940-48), Glen W. Maxwell (1949-51), R. H. Shaw (1952), Ernest Reid (1953). **Amethyst Ferry:** Names not found. **Antonsen's Ferry:** Carl Antonsen (1926)? **Athabasca Landing Ferry:** John Tyndall (1911), William Cole (1914)?, Robert Vance (1915)?, G. Devlin (1916-19), Christopher Johnson (1920), Arthur Cook (1925-26), M. Blair (1927), W. Gorman, S. Beattie, John Ehmig, T. E. Hillson, C. A. Ryder, T. Donohue (1928-35), D. Garton, C. A. Ryder, A. C. Pittman (1936-40), R. C. Davidson, A. C. Pittman (1941), D. Garton, A. C. Pittman, W. G. Reed, A. L. Webb (1942-45), Rosario LaPorte, G. T. Monson, D. W. Wain (1946), D. Garton, J. G. Owens, Fred Noakes, Walter Peters (1947-48), Walter Peters, M. McKay, Jack Rhodes, G. D. Rogers, George Malone, A. H. Webb (1949-51). **Atlee Ferry:** Names not found.

Banff Ferry: David Keefe (1884)?. **Bassano Ferry:** Operated by the public. **Battle River Ferries:** Abraham Salveis (Solway) (ca. 1885), George and Norman Smith (1902), Al Jeglum and Noah McCombs (1907), Hiram Brody Wood (1908), Ralph Smith (early 1900s). **Beaver Lake Ferry:** Joseph McCallum (1902-?). **Beauvallon Ferry:** Moise Donie (1932-1945), John Rutkowski (1946), Fred Popowich and Steve Trach (1947-49), Harry Taschuk (1950-51), Fred Popowich (1952-55), William Kostyniuk (1956), Mike Popowich (1957-58). **Beaver Crossing Ferry:** Albert Limoges (1911-?), Joseph Dery (1916-18). **Belvedere Ferry:** Gordon MacDonald (1898-?), Johnny Foley (?-1904), Morgan Buck (1904-12). **Berrymoor Ferry:** Frank Lewis (1916), Bob Fitzgerald (1917-24)?, James M. Plank (1925), George Crocombe (1926-46), Dick Cropley (1941), E. L. Gheseger (1947), Carroll Ward (1948-54), L. B. Roll, Carroll Ward (1955), William Delorey, Ira Haight (1956-58), Howard Cartwright, John Nixon (1958-64), J. D. Green, O. Johnston (1965), Berthold Laiss (1966-83) with J. Bowie (1966-67), Gerald Roberts (1968-69), Charlie Case (1970-72), John Reznick (1973), Edward Fewster (1974), Henry Schadek (1975-76), Henry Schadek, T. McDonnell (1977), Schadek, McDonnell, Tim Hutchinson (1978), Schadek, Hutchinson, Mark Paul (1979), Steven and Robin Stuhl, Stan Sunderland (1980), S. Stuhl, Walter Vannot, S. Sunderland (1981-83). **Bindloss Ferry**: Richard Krenbrenk (1956), Sam Helfrich (1957), Harold Moore, Lorne Schlact (1958-59), J. L. Callaghan, Lorne Schlact (1960), Lorne Schlact, William Bicknell (1961). **Blakeley Ferry**: The Blakeley family (ca. 1951-77).

Blue Ridge Ferry: Dave Webster (1919-26), Howard Knott (1927), L. Redmond (1930-35), Dave Webster (1936-52), Fred Harris (1953-60), Fred Harris, Walter Brazel (1961), G. Meads, Walter Brazel (1962), Walter Brazel, Harry Moser (1963-64), Walter and James Brazel (1965-68), James Brazel, Harry Moser (1969), James Brazel, Fred Baxandall, William Jackson (1970), Percy Benson (1971-77) with Ray Duncan (1971), Ray Duncan, Fred Baxandall (1972), Ray Duncan, Frank Underwood (1973), Frank Underwood, Ewald Schulz (1974-76), Ewald Schulz, A. Adams (1977). **Bow Island Ferry**: Charlie Barkman (n.d.), S. M. Hanna (1925-27), George Anger (1928-29), J. S. Ross (1930-40), A. C. Garrison (or Harrison) (1941-44), M. E. Neilson (1945-59), J. E. Atkinson (1951), Dan McGregor (1952-53), Adolf Wutzke (1954), John Hoel (1955-68) with Charles Casper and Joseph Schmidt. **Bow Slope Ferry**: Charles Goddard (1925-40), R. H. Westwong (1941-42), Dai Turner (1943), Engvold Johnson (1944), Carl Meier (1945), J. W. McPherson (1946-57), S. A. Welet (1948-49), William McKay (1950-54), William Murray (1955), R. N. Bacon, John Erb (1956), John Erb, Art Perry (1957), Ernest Alexson, Henry Pirker (1958). **Brosseau Ferry**: Mathias Lambert (1904-10), Antoine Brault, Frank Lapierre, Johnny Foisey, Frank Plouffe (n.d.), Azarie Venne (1911), Basil Theroux (1925-28), M. Blair (1929), J. Archambault (1930). **Buffalo Crossing Ferry**: Names not found.

Calgary Ferries: Cpl. Ralph Bell, S. Fogg, T. N. Willing, George Hamilton, W. G. Compton, Alfred McKay (n.d.). **Canmore Ferry**: Names not found. **Carcajou Ferry**: Names not found. **Carseland Ferry**: Tom Devine (1908-20), Alex Yuill, V. Hogg, Allen Mitchell, Denny Donovan, Ernie Wyndham (n.d.). **Chin Ferry**: Names not found. **Clover Bar Ferry**: Charles F. Stewart (1883-1903)?. **Coaldale Ferry**: Joe Pellerin, William Whitely (1910-13). **Colles Ferry**: H.J.C. Colles (1898). **Content Ferry**: Names not found. **Cosmo Ferry**: Names not found. **Cowley Ferry**: Mr. Bouthillier (ca. 1898). **Crooked Lake Ferry**: Adolph Rupertus (early 1900s)?. **Crooked Rapids Ferry**: Amable Paradis (1896-?). **Crowfoot Ferry**:

G. E. Cottingham (1925-27), G. W. Yates (1928-30), H. Greenwood (1931-42), Sig Carlson (1943-49), R. G. Wagar (1950-51), Caesar Devos (1952-62), G. A. Ernst (1963-64), A. Blackwater (1965-66), Edgar Littke (1967-72), Don Mancell (1973), Wayne Jones (1974-79), Lily Solway (1978-79), Bettey Wilken (1978-84), Larry Unrau (1979-84), Jack Wanamaker (1980-84), Raymond Badgley (1982-83), Ralph Teleford (1982).

Desjarlais Ferry: Charles Tillapaugh (n.d.), Milo Strynadka (1925), A. J. Melnychuk (1926), Mike Tkachuk (1927-28), A. J. Melnychuk (1929-30), Nick Rawliuk (1931), Metro Kureluk (1932-33), Milo Strynadka (1934-35), William Esak (1936-41), A. Albiston, W. M. Strynadka (1942), Theo Melnychuk, W. M. Strynadka (1943), Alex Melnychuk, A. N. West (1944), Alex Melnychuk, William Farris (1945), Alex Melnychuk, Paul Mynzak (1946), Paul Mynzak (1947-48), Paul Mynzak, J. H. Hawreliak (1949-51), J. Hawreliak, W. Ewaniuk (1952), G. A. Russ, Peter David (1953), Mike Tkachuk, Dan Nickoruk (1954-55), Dan Nickoruk, John Koroluk (1956-60) with Nick Shapka (1956) and William Elchuk (1957-60), John Koreluk, William Elchuk, George Russ (1961). **Dead Lodge Canyon Ferry:** Names not found except H. G. Jackson (n.d.) **Dorothy Ferry:** Paddy Fullerton (1906), Percy McBeath (1907-16)?, Sid Reeves, Bill LeBeau, Jesse Smith, John Duthoya (1917-24), George Scorgie (1925-42), Andrew Black (1943-44), Fred Pugh (1945-72), Gerry Gammie (1973-75).

Drayton Valley Ferry: Robert Bradford (1954), Robert Landers (1955), Robert Bradford, Robert Landers and Russell Davis (1956-57) with assistant ferrymen Steve Fillinger, Ernie Sass, Bob Ross, Deodat Lorimer, Len McGhee, W. M. McDermott, Bob Landers Jr. **Drumheller Ferries:** Thomas Greentree (1902), Jake Leonhardt (ca. 1909), Robert Wigmore (ca. 1907), James Russell (n.d.). **Dunvegan Ferry:** Joe Bissett (1909-24)?, P. J. Foster (1925-32) with A. Holmquist (1930), H. Y. Nicholson (1931-32), George Bennett, D. P. Smith (1933-35), D. P. Smith (1936-39), J. G. Kerr, H. Carmichael (1940), D. P. Smith, David Wilson (1941-42), D. Wilson, Harold DeWinter (1943), D. Wilson, George Foster (1944), D. Wilson, C. J. Whelan (1945-46), Otto Sorley, W. D. Lenn (1947), D. Wilson, Steve Schudlo (1948), Otto Sorley, Steve Schudlo (1949), Steve Schudlo, John Gronval (1950-51), J. D. Cadenhead, J. Gronval, J. Downie, Steve Schudlo (1952), J. Gronval, S. Schudlo, A. Gronval, M. J. McLeod, S. Sawchuk, Holger Peterson, Otto Sorley, J. Skaley, W. Hanson, H. Graham, Nick Schudlo, John Radomski, Mike Shmyruk (1953-60). **Durlingville Ferry:** Names not found.

East Coulee Ferry: A. C. Shanks (1930-40) with Al Duke (1936-37),

Tom Skevington (1938-40), S. Marham (1938-39), J.A.R. Lowe (1940), J.A.R. Lowe, Thomas Wilson (1941), Thomas Wilson (1942-46) with A. Beveridge (1942), H. R. Dowdle (1943-46), H. R. Dowdle, Cesar Devos (1947-49), Alex Zarooban, Ernest Grose (1950). **Edmonton Ferries:** Dan and Johnny McPhaden (1882-?), Mr. Gowler, Mr. Durdle, Mr. Fife, Mr. Murphy, Mr. Irvine, William Humberstone, and John Walter (n.d.). **Edson-Grande Prairie Trail Ferries:** Mr. Severson (1911-18), John Anderson, Mr. Ritchie (n.d.). **Eldorena Ferry:** Ernie Domshy (n.d.), Nick Sawchuk (1925-30), H. S. Chorney (1931-35), William Sikora (1936-38) with Mack Popil (1938), William Pawlechko (1939-41) with Alex Wintoniak (1939), William Sikora (1940), Mike Yarmola (1941), William Sikora, Mike Prokopy (1942), William Sikora, Kost Bodnar (1943), Elko Antosko, Panko Mulyk (1944), Paul Wolanski, Panko Mulyk (1945), William Shkolny (1946-48) with Mike Yarmola (1946), Panko Mulyk (1947-48), Elko Antosko, Panko Mulyk (1949), Panko Mulyk (1950-55) with Elko Antosko (1950-52) and Andrew Rasko (1953-55), William Kapitski (1956-61) with Andrew Rasko (1956-59), and Steve Sekersky (1960-61), Nick Mendiuk, S. Sekersky (1962-64), Mike Melnyk, S. Sekersky (1965-67).

Elk Point Ferry: Charlie Hood (1909-12), Charlie Magnusson (1913-16), George Bartling (n.d.), Bill Kellar (n.d.), O. M. Jacobson (1925-29), O. M. Jacobson, George Bartling (1930), Alf J. Monkman (1931-37) with I. H. Gilpin (1931), Paul Gusnowski (1932-33), William Keller, R. Mulholland (1934), D. J. McKay (1935), Harry Keck (1936-37), Harry Keck (1938-44) with A. J. Monkman (1938), Ernest Scott (1940-41), E. A. Vaughan (1942-43), Patrick Madden (1944), Paul Gusnowski, John Pankow (1945), William Rutherford, Frank Chuklinski, Henry Beaudette (1946), Gerald Stults, Onesim Lakusta, and George Boratynec (1947), Onesim Lakusta (1948-50) with G. Boratynec and P. Gusnowski (1948), P. Gusnowski, John Libich (1949), Alex Gusnowski and John Libich (1950). **Emerson Ferry:** Names not found. **Empress Ferries: West,** John Northcott (1913): William Englebrecht (prior to 1913)?. **East,** Allie Fjeldberg (n.d.). **South,** George Turner (1916-20), George Durk (1920-23), Hugh Miller (1924-56) with Stanley Hay (1935-42), Mike Ebelher (1943), Henry Hensel (1944), R. H. Imes (1945), W. R. Turner (1946), Emil Kovitch (1947), Martin Helfrich (1948-56), Martin Helfrich, J. L. Watson (1957), Martin Helfrich, Chris Helfrich (1958-61). **Entwistle Ferry:** Names not found. **Eunice Ferry:** Henry Weizel (ca. 1915)?. **Eyremore Ferry:** John Erickson (n.d.), W. H. Moore (prior to 1911).

Falher Ferry: Arthur St. Pierre (1947-53) with Phillipe Dechambre (1952), Oden Blagen (1953), Napoleon Paul, Alger Bellerose (1954),

Alfred Smith, Harvey Rivard (1955), Henry Squires, Leslie Howie (1956), Yvon Arnaud (1957-61) with Jeannot Simard (1957), J. C. Lacourse, Max Lefrancos, Lyster Dufour (1958), with August Audet, Raymond Fontaine (1959-61), with Emile Bachand, Edward Cloutier (1962), with Clarence Morin, Roy Jackson, G. Driver, and M. Leganchuk (1963). **Fawcett Ferries: West,** Joe Dawkins (1928-46), Howard Roberts, A. Sutton (1947), T. L. Bouvette (1948-50). **South,** H. C. Bell (1921-23)?, August Fangue (1924), J. L. Pumphrey (1925), E. F. Tyerman (1926), W. T. Goodwin (1936-42), Bernard Henry (1943), Paul Rockart (1944), A. L. Moser (1945-50). **Finnegan Ferry:** John Finnegan (n.d.), D. McLeod (1925-28), L. Mansell (1929), O. T. Olson (1930-47), Carl Anderson (1948-50), J. W. McPherson (1951-52), Louis Braconnier (1953), S. Carlson (1954), Walter Birce (1955-56), William J. Christiansen (1957-64), Frank Dale (1965-73), W. E. Murray (1974), Elmer McBride (1975-76), E. McBride, Bernard Hiebert (1978-81), Mr.McBride, Mr. Hiebert, and Hugh McGavin (1982), Mr. McBride and Mr. McGavin (1983-84). **Flatbush Ferry:** Edward Roper (1932-48), with R. Riddle (1944); J. J. Marshall (1949), F. C. Richardson (1950-51), J. G. Richardson (1952-55), Alios Sauter (1956).

Forbesville Ferry: Mr. Forbes, Billy Dumont, Tom Revard, Bill McCusker (n.d.), S. J. Kelliker (1925-26), Resiel Hawkins (1927-28), R. Roberton (1929-44), Resiel Hawkins (1945-49), C. W. Hayes (1950), John Forbes (1951-52), Ian Forbes (1953-54), William Roberton (1955-60). **Fort Kipp Ferry:** William Long and Richard Urch (n.d.). **Ford Macleod Ferry:** Names not found. **Fort Saskatchewan Ferry:** Joseph Lamoureaux (1874-1896). **Fort Vermilion Ferry:** H. A. McCord (1925-26), Leon Eauclaire (1927-45), Archie Mercredi (1946-55) with Herman Mercredi (1952), Daniel Ducharme (1954-55), Ken Tucker (1956) with A. Mercredi, William Charles, and Alger Bellerose (n.d.), H. Squires, A. Mercredi, B. M. Squires and Glen Openshaw (1957), A. Mercredi, Eric Flett, Chester Charles, John Elias and Daniel Hudson (1958-59), Mr. Mercredi, Mr. Flett, Mr. Charles, and Mr. Hudson (1959), H. R. MacKinnon, Mr. Mercredi, Mr. Charles, and Mr. Flett (1960), Clint Bundy (1961) with Ervin Halwas, Clifford Flett, and Frank Cook; Clint Bundy with C. H. Messenger, Jake Martin, and Russell Hofford (1962), Holger Pedersen with Wilhelm Fehr, Jake Martin, Lindy Paul, C. H. Messenger, W. E. Lizotte (1963), E. Halwas, J. L. Peters, L. Paul, and P. F. Schmidt (1964), W. Fehr, J. F. Schmidt, J. L. Peters and L. Paul (1965), (1963-65), Wilhelm Fehr (1966), R. Lambert, J. F. Schmidt, W. Lizotte, L. Paul, and P. F. Schmidt; William Fehr (1967), L. Paul, P. Schmidt, Robert Lambert, A. Mercredi, J. Schmidt, A. S. Lizotte (1968) with L. Paul,

J. Schmidt, R. Lambert, W. R. Friesen, A. Mercredi, Harvey Flett; A. L. Lizotte (1969), H. Flett, J. Schmidt, Jake Friesen, Norman Lizotte, A. Mercredi, Louie Dumas; Harvey Flett (1970), J. Schmidt, N. Lizotte, Angus Peters, A. Mercredi, L. Dumas, Russell Paul; Norman Lizotte (1971), J. Schmidt, Dennis Smith, Ernest Mercredi, A. Mercredi, L. Dumas, Einar Malmquist; Edward Lizotte (1972), E. Mercredi, A. Mercredi, J. Schmidt, John Zacharias, L. Dumas, Frank Wiebe.

Garrington and Niddrie Ferries: Reuben Rambo, Fred Aldridge, George and Gorman Overguard, Lowell Meissner, Bill Ross, Christian Nelson (n.d.), E. R. Meissner (1925-54), with David Thomas (1936), Ralph Cove (1937), David Thomas (1938-40), Lester Johnson (1952), Maurice Cheston (1953-54), Maurice Cheston (1955-58) with L. T. Meissner (1955), Lester Johnson (1956-58), Lester Johnson, Alvin Johnson (1959-60), Alvin Johnson and Laurence P. James (1961-62). **Genesee, Cropley and Scheideman Ferries:** Cropley and Scheideman families (1906-17), Hugo Neiman (1919-?), James Greenhough (1925-35), George Akins (1936-40), P. S. Irvine (1941-46), S. G. Irvine (1947-48), Ernest Sass (1949-54) with Keith Lowe (1952), T. Nesjan (1953), and Joe Enedy (1954), T. M. Nesjan (1955-61) with Louis Nesjan (1955-56), Edward Nesjan (1957-58), John Akins (1959), Leonard Karlson (1960-61), Fred Harris and Frank Mahony (1962), Berthold Laiss (1963-65) with Benny Weiss (1963-64) and J. Nesjan (1965). **Goodwin Ferry:** Goodwin brothers (1910 own ferry), Pat McCann (1916), James Kimmerley (1925-30), William Moody (1931-42) with A. E. Tomlin (1934-35), Fred Sedore (1936-42); Reg Moody (1943-49) with Fred Sedore and C. E. Calberry (1943-44), Clayton Calberry (1945), C. Calberry and T. M. Stark (1946-47), C. Calberry and M. L. McCrady (1948), C. Calberry and Fred Sedore (1949). **Grassy Lake Ferry:** Operated by the public. **Gregory Crossing Ferry:** Jim Gregory (1913-?), H. S. Schofield, Bill Hosler (n.d.), J. Dancker (1925), F. H. McCaughey (1926-27), Reuben Smith (1928), C. Dancker (1929-35), R. A. (Alf) Bradshaw (1936-60). **Grouard Ferry:** Names not found. **Grovedale Ferry:** Otto Sorley (1934-44), Edward Gates (1945), Otto Sorley (1946), H. L. Brown (1947), James Kimmerley (1948-58) with C. W. Gabler (1956-57), and Ed Yates (1958), Alvin Johnson (n.d.).

Hazel Bluff Ferry: Andrew Jenner (n.d.)?. **Heinsburg Ferry:** Albert Winkler (1914-16), Gilbert (Gib) Evans (1917-22) with Gus Clack, Gus Maas, Ole Johanson (n.d.) John Nichols (1923-25), J. O. Johnson (1927-29), Gilbert Evans (1930-43) with Charles Gibson (1930), W. L. Crook (1931), G. Gunderson (1932), W. L. Crook (1933-35), F. Kjenner (1936), W. L. Crook (1937-39), Ralph Crook

(1941-42), Eric Sharkey and Lester Botting (1943), W. L. Crook (1944-48), with Steve Sawak (1944-45), J. Maksymiuk and Nick Bakala (1946), J. Maksymiuk and Gib Evans (1947), J. Maksymiuk and T. W. Crook (1948), John Maksymiuk (1949-50), with Walter Sawak and L. B. Blakely (1949), W. Sawak and Mike Stojanowski (1950), B. C. Edwards, W. Sawak, and George Bottling (1951), Walter Sawak (1952-63) with G. Bottling, J. E. Nichols (1952), Oscar Vinge and J. E. Nichols (1953), J. E. Nichols (1954), J. S. Nichols and Carrol Fraser (1955-58), O. Vinge and Mike Chmilar (1959), O. Vinge and G. Botting (1961-62), O. Vinge and Frank Sikora (1963). **High River Ferry**: Jasper (Buck) Smith (1886-?).

Hinton Ferry: J. R. McNeeley (1914-?), W. M. McLeod (1916-?). **Holborn Ferry**: Frank Suter, Sam Everington, Ed Halla, Tom Scott (n.d.), L. Washburn (1925), J. Gibson (1926), L. Washburn (1927), A. W. Crane (1928-29), C. R. Meads (1930-31), Carl Propp (1932-35), G. W. Scott (1936), C. R. Meads (1937-41), W. N. Meads (1942), C. R. Meads (1943-58), G. Meads (1959-61), T. M. Nesjan (1962-64). **Holmes Crossing Ferry**: William Holmes (1905-12), Guy Stuart (1913-21), Wesley Cartwright (1922-42), with Frank Dabels (from 1938), Frank Dabels and Marvin Coley (1943-44), Anton Dabels and Ray Olson (1945), Ray Olson and Eldred Baxter (1946), Ray Olson and Nolton Cartwright (1947), C. W. Cartwright and Dutee Cartwright (1948-51), Dutee Cartwright (1952-56) with G.C. Cartwright and Hugh English (1952), J. B. Erskine and H. E. Cartwright (1953), J. B. Erskine and Austin Kepke (1954), Austin and Walter Kepke (1955-56). **Hopkins Ferry**: J. H. Earle (1914), Carl Otto (1916), A. D. McGinnis (1925-36), P. Martin (1937-41), Leon Kobel (1942-45), Nick Zakaruck (1946), Leon Kobel (1947-48), Carl Nelson (1949), Leon Kobel (1950-70). **Houk Ferry**: George Houk, Mr. Layton (1870-?). **Hutton Ferry**: Field brothers (n.d.), E. "Irish" Mellon (1925-36), J. J. Tyler (1937-40), R. H. Imes (1941-46), Carl Anderson (1947), Merlin Suitor (1948-49), ? (1950-51), James Freeguard (1952), Clarence McNeil (1953-58), Henry Pirker (1959-60).

Jarvie Ferry: Names not found. **Jenner Ferry**: Frank Sussman (1925-40), Ira German (1941-59), Louis Pelchat (1960-64), O. Pancoast (1965-66), Herbert J. Line (1967-69), Vilho Matson (1970-77), Edwin Aebbley and Bruce Steggan (1978-80) with David Riste (1980).

Kinuso Ferry: Names not found. **Klondike Ferry**: G. J. Fowler (1932-36), Horace Sebern (1937-46), Andrew Park, C. W. Cartwright (1947), Nolton Cartwright (1948-50), George Mansoff (1951-65), Ted Dabels (1966-70), Garth Neumann (1971-81), Albert Voight and Gilbert Branden (1971-81), G. Neumann, A. Voight, G. Branden, with

Erwin Witzke (1982), C. Neumann, A. Voight, Mr. Witzke and William Kuric (1983-84).

Lac Ste. Anne Ferry: Stony Indian known as "Weezaw" (Oiseau) (1905-07?), H. H. Jones (1925-57), Berthold Laiss (1958-62). **La Corey Ferry:** Frank Levesque (n.d.). **La Crete Ferry:** J. Grinval and Holger Pedersen (1962), J. Schapansky, P. F. Peters, D. F. Marten, J. H. Peters, J. L. Peters (1963-64), J. D. Schellenberg with J. Buhler, J. Alais, P. Wall, B. K. Goertzen, J. H. Derksen, P. F. Peters, William Friesen, J. Teichrob (1965-66), John Buhler (1967-73) with Mr. Friesen, Pete Zacharias, Jacob Neufeld, John Klassen, Peter Fehr (1967), with P. Weiler, Mr. Zacharias, Mr. Neufeld, Mr. Alais, Mr. Fehr, and Mr. Goertzen (1968), with Mr. Wieler, Mr. Zacharias, Mr. Neufeld, Mr. Alais and Mr. Goertzen (1969), with Mr. Wieler, Mr. Zacharias, Mr. Neufeld, Mr. Alais, Mr. Goertzen, Mr. Schellenberg, George Janzen, and Jacob Petkau (1970), with Mr. Wieler, Mr. Teichrob, Mr. Janzen, Mr. Petkau, and Dave Dreidger (1971), with Mr. Neufeld, Mr. Petkau, Mr. Janzen, and Mr. Teichrob (1972), with Mr. Teichrob, Mr. Petkau, Mr. Buhler Jr. and Abraham Weiler (1973), Jacob Teichrob (1974-76) with Jacob Klassen, Jacob Reddekop, Jacob Neustater, John Friesen, Jacob Petkau, Herman Bueckert, Jacob Schmidt, J. Schmidt (1977), Mr. Bueckert, and A. & J. Friesen, Mr. Petkau, Mr. Neustater, and J. Krahn; Herman and Jacob Buechert (1978-79).

Lea Park Ferry: Louis Patenaude (1908), David Bristow (1910)?, Dolphus Nolan (1911)?, Swan Johnson (1912-14), Helge Berg, Knut Johnson, Frank Jacobs (n.d.), Ole Tweed (1925), W. J. Maas (1926-28), Oscar Fleming (1929), Oscar Fleming, E. Helgerson and N. B. Horness (1930), Ole Tweed (1931-41) with E. Helgerson (1931-36) and Martin Grasdal (1937-41), M. Grasdal and O. Vinge (1942), M. Grasdal and Ed Klinkner (1943), Ed. Klinkner and T. Hyatt (1944-45), T. Hyatt and W. G. Hyatt (1946), M. Grasdal, E. T. Hyatt and N. B. Norness (1947), M. Grasdal, Mr. Horness, and Mr. Hyatt (1948-57), with P. Mulyk (1948-49), Elko Antosko (1950-52), and Andrew Rasko (1953-57). **Lethbridge Ferry:** Nick Sheran (?-1882), Edward Sutherland (1883-84). **Lett's Crossing Ferry:** J. S. Calder (1926-27), G. W. Kidney (1928-35), Scott Durling (1935), F. Johnson (1936-39), W. Tennant (1940-50), W. LeRoy Cole (1951-53), Robert Cole (1954), Fred Baxandall (1955-65). **Lindbergh Ferry:** John Chilbeck and Walter Soper (n.d.), Henry Anderson (1925-27), Archie Anderson (1928), Henry Anderson (1929-32), William Jurak (1933), Henry Anderson (1934-35), Neal Edwards (1936-39), James Madden (1940-48), with Fred Madden (1948), Steve Sawak and Clifford Stults (1949), Steve Sawak and Lawrence Sharkey (1950), Gerald and Clifford Stults (1951), Richard Ingersol (1952), Harry Kalynchuk (1953), Rolf Anderson (1954-62). **Lunnford Ferry**: Frank Pringle and J. S. Calder (n.d.).

McKenzie Ferry: Roderick and David McKenzie (1883-?). **McLeod Valley Ferry**: Hank Tomlinson (1913)?, J. Fairholm (1925-30), B. N. Fairholm (1931-34), F. J. Smith (1936-37), F. J. Smith (1938-50) with P. W. Young (1938-40), Gordon Jacobs (1942-45), L. B. Rolls (1946-47), A. P. Shand (1948-49), L. B. Rolls (1950), L. B. Rolls (1951-54) with A. Shand, P. W. Young, H. H. Tomlinson, F. A. Radcliffe; H. H. Tomlinson, and David Jenkins (1955). **McNeil Ferry**: Edward McNeil (ca. 1920-?).

Mahaska Ferry: Tom Fallon and Bill Jones (n.d.) James Cunningham (1924), Harry Hellekson (1925), James Scott (1926-30), James Milner (1931-47), C. C. Kinney (1948), Lloyd Larsen (1950-51), Robert Bradford (1952-53). **Majeau Lake Ferry**: Torvald Nelson (1936). **Manola Ferry**: Wilbur Clarke (1925-26)?. **Matthews Crossing Ferry**: M. H. Matthews, (1914-18), Mr. Balfour (1919), Tom Pearce (1920-27), M. H. Lawrence (1928), F. T. Harris (1929-31), J. Anderson (1932), F. T. Harris (1933-37). **Medicine Hat Ferry**: T. N. Willing (1883); "Long Day" (1884-89): W. R. Johnston (1900-1902). **Meridian Ferry**: Fred Hallett (n.d.) G. A. Montan (1926-26), John Martinson (1927-28), F. W. McAllister (1929), Jack Ellis (1930-33), R. D. Bezanson (1934-41), N. J. Ricard (1942-53), L. J. Hewitt (1954-59), P. N. Postnikoff, D. Ward, C. Foulds, E. Menslaff, William Pierce (1960-?). **Milk River Ferries**: Mr. Satterlee and Mr. Fitzmaurice (n.d.). **Mirror Landing Ferry**: Ed Brazeau (1925-26), John Brazeau (1927-28), Jack Mischkow (1929), Mose Villeneuve and John Zubach (1930), Mose Villeneuve and Tegner Nohr (1931), John Brazeau and Bert Ramsay (1932-33) Alex McDonald (1934-42) with Dan McPherson (1934-40) George Brown (1941), M. Villeneuve (1942). **Mitford Ferry**: Names not found. **Monarch Ferry**: F. R. Dalzell (1909). **Morley Ferry**: Names not found. **Morrin Ferry**: Fred Clegg (1913-15), Alex Stauffer (1916), E. Tupper Fisher (1917-21), F. Apps (1921-26), O. Dancker (1927), C. Dancker (1928), R. Smith (1929), Charles Hatton (with Tom Miller and Tom Miller Jr. ?) (1930-37), Charles Hatton and J. H. Smith (1938-40), C. Lewis and Tom Skevington (1941), Frank Davis and T. Skevington (1942), Tom Skevington (1943-45) with Albert Hiller (1943), Alex Cooper (1944), Frank Davis (1945), J. H. Smith and T. Skevington (1946-50), J. H. Smith and William Falconer (1951-59).

Mountain House Ferry: Names not found. **Munson Ferry**: Andre Bleriot (1913-24), Emil Perreal, Magnus Johnson, Tommy Johnson,

174

Andy Sutherland, Silas Dunham (n.d.), W. Johnston (1925-26), J. S. Tucker (1927-31), J. S. Tucker and C. Lewis (1932), C. Lewis (1933-37), C. Lewis and B. Miller (1938-40), William Henderson (1941-45), E. F. Davis (1946), William Henderson (1947-54), J. D. Lynch (1955-56), Homer Lee (1957), John Jacobson (1958-64), Lloyd Heaton and J. D. Lynch (1965-72), David Brown and A. Tulli-kopf (1973), David Brown Kenneth Hill and Cyril Nelson (1974), Cyril Nelson, J. Delaney, V. McKnight, and C. Dimmer (1975-77), Mr. Delaney, Mr. Nelson, and Mr. Dimmer (1978), Mr. Delaney, Mr. Nelson, Mr. Dimmer and Jim Carlson (1979-80), Mr. Delaney, Mr. Nelson, Mr. Carlson, and Clem Hamelin (1981), Mr. Delaney, Mr. Hamelin, and Mark Patterson (1982), Mr. Delaney, Mr. Hamelin, and George Smith (1983), Mr. Delaney, Mr. Smith and Victor Malinowski (1984). **Myrnam Ferry:** Nick Bodnar, George Hultash, Mr. Boha-chyk, Mr. Prill, and Al Maksymiuk (n.d.), D. Maksymiuk (1925-26), George Forchuk (1927-32), A. Lockton (1933-35), Onesim Lakusta (1936-46) with N. P. Luityk, Sam Saganeuk, and C. Krankowsky; Joseph Lecapoy (1947-53) with Nick Kish, Byl Zacharuk, and Pete Tymofichuk; George Borotynec (1954-69) with Byl Zacharuk, Alex Yakimowich, and Bill and Joe Tymofichuk; Alex Yakimowich and Charles Krankowsky (1970).

Oliver Ferry: Names not found.

Pancreas Ferry: Mr. DeForest, Alex La Tromboise (n.d.). **Peace River Crossing Ferry:** Walter Mellish (1911).

Red Deer Ferry: Sage Bannerman (1883-1893?). **Riverbow Ferry:** Colin Dick (1925), William Levette (1928-38). **Rocky Buttes Ferry:** Names not found. **Rolling Hills Ferry:** Jacob Harder (1955-56), Carl Engel and Robert Holmes (1958-72), Robert Holms and John Greer (1973), E. J. McBride and Walter Degenstein (1974). **Rocky Moun-tain House Ferry:** Burl Gray (1908-1916), O. E. (Opie) Thompson (1917-42) with H. Thompson (1930-33), R. Young (1934), A.L.P. Gib-son (1935-37), A. Van Dyke (1938-40), J. J. Richards (1941), Fred Begnold (1942), T. W. Gray and L. H. Prowse (1943), T. W. Gray and W. Spurgeon (1944), W. Spurgeon, N. Dick and Dan Cross (1945). **Rosedale Ferry:** E. Tuckwood (1925), P. J. Sullivan and L. Mason (1926), P. J. Sullivan (1927-28), C. Hatton (1929), A. Anderson (1930-42) with H. Upton (1930), R. Cunningham (1931-36), A. Higden and C. R. Ulm (1937), C. R. Ulm (1938-41), W. Dowdle (1942), G. E. Evans, Eric Sharkey and Chester Botting (1943), J.A.R. Lowe and W. Dowdle (1944-45), W. Dowdle, C. Devos, and N. Arend (1947). **Rose-vear Ferry:** W. G. Claridge (1925), E. J. Claridge (1926-39), G. Dixon (1940-42), J. D. Nicholson (1943-52), Mike Iwanciwski (1953-74) with William Iwanciwski (1958-65), A. Verpaelst and Alvin Wegert (1966),

Steve Eleniak (1967-68), Fred Baxandall (1969), Alvin Wegert (1970-74), Ludwig Busch (1973), and T. Shannon (1974), Floyd Radcliffe, Mr. Wegert and T. Shannon (1975), Alvin Wegert and Tom Shannon (1976), Mr. Wegert, Mr. Shannon, and F. Radcliffe (1977-79), Mr. Wegert, Mr. Shannon, Mr. Radcliffe, and Meredith L'Hirondelle (1980-81), Mr. Wegert, Mr. Radcliffe, Mr. L'Hirondelle, and Kevin Holloway (1982), Mr. Wegert, Mr. Radcliffe, Mr. L'Hirondelle, Mr. Holloway, and William Baudin (1983), Mr. Wegert, Mr. Radcliffe, Mr. Holloway, and John Horvath (1984).

St. Paul Ferry: Mathias Lambert (ca. 1904). **Sandy Lake Ferry**: Names not found. **Sangudo Ferry**: Frank Wright, David Lowry (1925-36), F. B. Teer (1937-41), W. N. Brown (1943-44), Harry Popowich (1945-50). **Sawridge Ferry**: Names not found. **Shaftesbury Ferry**: O. Marceau (1978-84), Art Hammond (1978), Brian Neff (1978), Albert Jacob (1978), Richard Draeger (1978), J. Buehler (1978), Doug Bourque (1978), Gerard Marceau (1979-80), Diane Baglo (1979), Stanley Debogorski (1979-84), Frederick St. Germain (1979-80), Darryl Woods (1979), Debra Bzowy (1979-80), John Cowan (1979), Kenneth Williamson (1979-84), Ivan Glasier (1980-82), Gerard Langlois (1980-84), Leonard Tunke (1981), Nigel Ryan (1981), Henri Boivan (1981), Lloyd Bettenson (1981-84), and Murray Ellis (1982-84).

Shandro Ferry: Nicolai Moisey (1906-19), Gordon Haines (1920-25), Nick Chornohus and William Moisey (1926), William Hampton (1927-28), H. Doshownek (1929), A. J. Monkman and N. Hokiro (1930), Tom Hawreliak and John Tashchuk (1931), John Taschuk and John Huculiak (1932-33), Mike Tchachuk and Dave Klem (1934), Mike Tchachuk and William Poburan (1935), George Romanko and F. Shewchuk (1936-37), George Romanko and Alex Katerinchuk (1938-39), N. W. Radomsky, George Romanko and F. Shewchuk (1940), Alex Katerinchuk (1941-42) with George Romanko (1941), A. J. Farus (1942-43), George Shandro and A. J. Farus (1944), Alex Farus and George Doshewnek (1945-47), George Shandro (1948-54) with Metro Popowich (1948), Harry Dashiwnek (1949-51), Harry Dashiwnek and Metro Krawchuk (1952), Metro Krawchuk and Nick Repchuk (1953), Metro Krawchuk and Nick Radomsky (1954), Metro Krawchuk (1955-62) with Nick Radomsky and W. P. Chernichan (1955), W. P. Chernichan and Bill Katerinchuk (1956-60), Bill Katerinchuk and John Radomsky (1961-62).

Steerford Ferry: S. McKay (1909), H. E. England (1918), A. Mitchell (1919-22). **Steveville Ferry**: Steven Hall (1909-11) Ambrose Shaw (1912-28), C. Connors and F. B. Ertmold (1929-46), J. W. MacPherson (1947-50) with E. J. McBride (1947-48), V. Roper (1949-50), V. Roper (1951-56) with Alfred Kingston (1951), George Tommason

176

(1952), Claus P. Narum (1953-56); Claus P. Narum and Earl House (1957-60), R. A. (Alf) Bradshaw (1961-66) with Claus P. Narum (1961), Martin Helfrich (1962), Chris Helfrich (1963-66); Charles Helfrich and J. A. McBride (1967-69), Chris Helfrich and Victor Vanderloh (1970). **Summerview Ferry**: Jim Douglas (1906-07), Tom Elliott (1908-09), William Glass (1910-12), Charles LaFrance (1915), Oliver Jones (1917-18). **Sunniebend Ferry**: Les Short (1911), Jack Woodlet (1912-18), Bill Marshall (1919-21).

Taber Ferry: Names not found. **Taylor Flats Ferry**: Donald Herbert Taylor (1912-?). **Thornton Ferry**: Names not found except H. Tomlinson (1917). **Tindastoll Ferry**: Frank Thomson (1898-?) **Tolman Ferry**: Ted Postill, S. T. Thompson, and W. D. Lenn (n.d.), Tom Lynch with Tom Skevington (1951), Matt Mechefske (1952), Matt Mechefske and Lloyd Heaton (1953), Lloyd Heaton and R. McPherson (1954-55), Homer C. Lee (1956), and J. Lynch (1957-64).

Victoria Ferry; Louis Thompson (1892-1905), Samuel Whitford (1906), Names not available (1907-24), Mike Elchuk (1925-27), William Elchuk (1928), Metor Koroluk (1929-30), Harry Smerenka (1931), N. Hnatyshyn (1932-33), S. Popovich (1934-35), Ed Albiston (1936-40) with S. Meronyk (1938-39), and H. Pillott (1940), James Ostapowich and H. Pillott (1941), M. Tod, and H. Pillott (1942), Ed Albiston (1943-50) with William Tkachuk (1943), Alex Hamaliuk (1944-45), N. Meronyk (1946), Fred Hamaliuk (1947), Z. Sadoway (1948), Nick Bidniak (1949-50); Nick Bokanesky and Nick Bidniak (1951), William Kapitski (1952-55) with D. Stefiuk (1952), Thomas Rogers (1953), John Solowan (1954), Nick Repchuk (1955), George Kotyk (1956-66), with Nick Repchuk (1956-62), Metro Krawchuk (1963-64), W. Zmurchuk (1965-66); Metro Krawchuk (1967-72) with Nick Repchuk and George Alexandriuk. **Vinca Ferry**: William, Andrew and John Puchalik (n.d.), Andrew Holowach (1922-24), D. Manchuk (1925-30), John Koziak (1931-33), John Checknita (1934), P. Konsorado (1935), Nick Farion (1936-41), Dan Manchuk (1942-49), Earl Cromarty and John Worobec (1950), Onesim Lakusta (1951-56) with John Libich, John Worobec, and Andy Shand (1951), Tom Rogers and W. P. Young (1952), Steve Fedorak and H. H. Tomlinson (1953), Steve Fedorak, Nick Kuchan, and F. A. Radcliffe (1954), Steve Fedorak, Nick Kuchan, and David Jenkins, Jr. (1955-56), Steve Fedorak (1957-66); with Nick Kuchan and William Hunka (1957-61), William Hunka and Emile Chaba (1962), and William Hunka, Emile Chaba and J. D. Lynch (1963-66).

Warspite Ferry: Robert Sinclair (1925), Nick Osadchuk (1926-27), Dan Anderson (1928-39), N. Mendiuk and P. Hunka (1940), Steve Sadowy (1941), George ? (1942), Nick Mendiuk (1943), Mike Melnyk

(1944-63) with Nick Mendiuk (1952-61), Pete Ostapowich (1962), and William Tychkowsky (1963). **Waskatenau Ferry:** Fred Henson (1921-23), Asher Warr (1924-35), with Earl Toane (1930-35), C. H. Robinson (1936-37) with Henry Antosko (1936), B. Kuefler (1937); Henry Antosko (1938-39) with Alex Wintoniak (1938), George Woodward (1939); J. M. Pysmeny (1940-42), with Alex Antoniak (1940), Henry Antosko (1941), Steve Letersky (1942), Harry Pillott and Alex Dmyterko (1943), Kost Bodnar and A. Dmyterko (1944), William Shkolny and A. Dmyterko (1945), J. M. Pysmeny and Fred Sawschuk (1946), Kost Bodnar and Andrew Rasko (1947), Andrew Rasko (1948-49) with Pete Kostreva (1948), and Fred Shmata (1949), Kost Bodnar and Peter Repka (1950-51), Nick Osadchuk (1952-61) with Mike Tchir and Andrew Kapach (1952), W. Michaelewich and Mike Shatina (1953), George Kotyk and Sam Prusak (1954-55), Sam Prusak and Mike Rozak (1956-61), Sam Prusak (1962-63) with Mike Rozak and Joe Fednyiak.

Watino Ferry: O. Carbon and P. McCallum (1915), O. C. Kenney (1939), Fred Anderson (1942), R. M. McCammon (1943), Berger Aaserud, Chris Olden, G. A. Williams, and Fred Anderson (1944), B. Aaserud and Robert Scott (1945), T. M. Stark and Ray Colton (1946), B. Aaserud and Ray Colton (1947-49), J. W. Henry (1950). **Wembley Ferry:** Robert Shaw (1930-33), W. P. Henderson (1932-43), "Commodore" Ed Wood (1944-51), Robert McCullough (1952-54), Harold McCullough (1955-57) with Peter McCullough (1956-57), Harold McCullough and Ralph Hosker (1958-61), Leland Campbell and Theodore Savard (1962-68). **Whitecourt Ferry:** C. Brown (1923), John Willis (1924), Elmer Coackley (1925-27). **Wild Horse Ferry:** Charlie O'Neill and "Barny" Barnhouse (n.d.). **Wolf Creek Ferry:** Names not found.

Bibliography

Charles Napier Bell. "A Day with the Buffalo Hunters." *Alberta History,* Winter 1982, pp. 25-27.

John Burgon Bickersteth. *The Land of Open Doors.* London: W. Gardner, Darton, 1914.

John Blue. *Alberta, Past and Present.* Chicago: Pioneer Historical Publishing Co., 1924.

Edwin Clarence Guillet. *Early Life in Upper Canada.* Toronto: Ontario Publishing Co., 1933.

William Katherens. "Memoirs of a Ferry Construction Foreman 1936-60," manuscript. Provincial Archives of Alberta, Edmonton.

John McDougall. *Forest, Lake and Prairie.* Toronto: W. Briggs, 1895.

John McDougall. *George Millward McDougall, the Pioneer, Patriot and Missionary.* Toronto: W. Briggs, 1888.

Alexander Hugh McQuarrie. "Now It Can Be Told," manuscript. Glenbow Archives, Calgary.

Archibald McRae. *History of the Province of Alberta.* Calgary: Western Canada History Co., 1912.

William Fitzwilliam Milton, and W. B. Cheadle. *The North-West Passage by Land.* London: Cassell, Petter & Galpin, 1865.

G. Bernard Wood. *Ferries & Ferrymen.* London: Cassell & Company Ltd., 1969.

Reports:

Annual reports, North-West Mounted Police, 1874-97.

Annual reports, North-West Territorial Government, 1887-1905.

Reports and files, Alberta Department of Public Works.

Reports and files, Alberta Department of Transportation.

Reports and files, Alberta Transportation.

Ferry Ordinance of 1884

An Ordinance Respecting Ferries
(Passed 6th August, 1884)

BE IT ENACTED by the Lieutenant-Governor or the North-West Territories, in Council, as follows:

1. It shall be lawful for the Lieutenant-Governor at any time to issue a license to any person or persons for the establishment and usage of a ferry or ferries, upon any river or stream or navigable water in the North-West Territories, granting the exclusive right to ferry over the same during the time and within the limits specified and described in such license, and upon such terms, with such security and other arrangements as are hereinafter provided.

2. Such License shall:
   (1.)Not be granted for a longer term than three years;
   (2.)Nor for any greater limit than three miles up and three miles down stream from the point at which the ferry is to be placed, as specified in the license;
   (3.)Nor for any ferry other than such as may be known as a cable or swing ferry;
   (4.)Nor for any ferry of which the boat or scow is not of sufficient capacity to carry safely one double wagon loaded to the extent of three thousand pounds, with two horses or other draught animals attached.

3. The maximum rate of tolls which may be charged for each crossing by means of a licensed ferry, under the preceding sections of this Ordinance, shall be as follows:
   (1.)For any water six hundred feet wide, or over, at low water mark, at any point within the limits of the operation of the license, for every
   a. Double vehicle, loaded or unloaded, including two horses or other draught animals and driver, 50 cents;
   b. Vehicle loaded or unloaded, drawn by single horse or other animals, with driver, 25 cents;
   c. Horse or other animal, with rider, 20 cents;
   d. Horse, mule, ox or cow, without vehicle or rider, 5 cents;
   e. Passenger, other than the driver of any single or double vehicle, or the rider of any animal, 5 cents;
   f. Animal, more than two attached to any vehicle, 10 cents;
   g. Pig, sheep, colt, calf or dog, 5 cents;
   h. All articles or goods not in a vehicle, over one hundred pounds, per 100 pounds, 2 cents;
   i. Foot passenger, 10 cents.
   (2.)For any stream or water less than six hundred feet wide, as provided in the preceding portion of this section, three-fourths the rates specified in the next preceding subsections shall be the maximum rates that may be charged.

4. The fee to be paid by a licensee on receiving a ferry license as hereinafter provided shall be five dollars.

5. Notwithstanding anything contained in the pre-ceding sections of this Ordinance, and where ferry licenses do not exist, the Lieutenant-Governor may grant ferry licenses at rates and on terms and conditions other than those specified in the said preceding sections, and may make a charge for the granting of a ferry license over and above the amount specified in section four of this Ordinance, and the amount of such charge shall be determined in the manner following:
   (1.)An advertisement shall be inserted in the newspaper published nearest the point at which the ferry is to run, asking for tenders of a yearly bonus to be paid for the license to ferry on the water within the limits advertised and at the rates advertised, continuously for two months previous to the date up to which tenders will be received, and notices of similar effect shall be posted up conspicuously for the same period at or in the immediate vicinity of the point where it is proposed the ferry shall run;

(2.) Such advertisement and notice shall state the time, limits, rates, and terms that shall be contained in the license, as well as the security required, and the date and place and by whom, under the authority of the Lieutenant-Governor, the tenders shall be opened and awarded;

(3.) Tenders may state a different amount of bonus for each year, over which the license is advertised to extend, and such bonus shall be payable in equal monthly instalments at the end of May, June, July, August, September, and October, or such of these months as may be included in the time covered by the license;

(4.) At the time and place mentioned in the advertisement and notices, the person therefore appointed shall open the tenders and award the license to the person making the most satisfactory tender with satisfactory security, but in case none of the tenders are satisfactory, then none need be accepted;

a. The Lieutenant-Governor may advertise, as hereinbefore provided, that any such ferry license shall be sold by public auction, in which case the bonus shall be payable as hereinbefore provided, and such sale shall be conducted and license awarded according to the terms of the advertisement and notice of such sale.

6. The Lieutenant-Governor-in-Council, if such shall be deemed in the public interest, may grant a bonus to accompany a ferry license.

7. Licensed ferries shall be run at all hours of the day and night, Sundays included, at which they are required, unless in cases in which loss of life or injury to or loss of property is likely to result therefrom, but in every case in which a ferry is used after nine (9) o'clock in the evening or before six (6) o'clock in the morning, double the rates specified in the license of such ferry may be charged.

8. Notwithstanding anything contained elsewhere in this Ordinance no toll shall be charged on children going to or returning from school, and in no case

shall Her Majesty's mail be obstructed, or charged more than the rates that may be charged according to the terms of license between the hours of six o'clock in the morning and nine o'clock in the evening.

9. In case a stream, to ferry which a license has been granted, becomes too low to work such boat or scow, as provided in section two, sub-section four, the licensee shall keep a row boat or canoe, with which he shall transfer foot passengers and baggage across such stream.

10. The approaches to every ferry shall be kept in such condition by the licensee that such ferry shall be easily accessible at all times for loaded doble teams without danger of loss of or injury to property.

11. A ferry on any stream that may be fordable at any time shall not be used to block up or injure the ford or fords or landing from the usual ford or fords on such stream, nor shall the licensee do any act that shall in any reasonable degree make the fording of such stream any more difficult than it would have been without his having done such act.

12. The Lieutenant-Governor shall express and define in every ferry license granted the maximum rate of tolls, on payment of which persons and property shall be ferried over the river or stream within the limits to which such license applies, the kind and size of vessels to be used in such ferrying, the limits of river and length of time covered by such license and the provisions, reservations and liabilities provided in this Ordinance, shall apply to every such license.

13. It shall be the duty of every person holding a ferry license to keep at all times posted up in a conspicious place on both sides of the river, as near as possible to such ferry, a schedule or clear statement, certified by the Clerk of the North-West Council, showing the ferry rates and the hours of crossing.

14. The Lieutenant-Governor shall, from time to time, appoint ferry inspectors, not having any interest in such ferry as owner, surety or otherwise, whose duty it shall be to report on the condi-

181

tion of such ferry or infractions of this Ordinance by the licensee, from time to time as requested by the Lieutenant-Governor, or on complaint of any party using or desiring to use any such ferry.

15. And if at any time a person holding a ferry license fails to comply with the written directions of an inspector, by neglecting to repair or not removing a vessel condemned, or not providing a suitable vessel within the time specified in such direction, he shall forfeit his license.

16. Before any license granted as hereinafter provided shall take effect the licensee shall give to the Lieutenant-Governor a bond with one or more approved sureties, in a penal sum of one thousand dollars, conditioned for the faithful performance of the conditions hereinbefore set forth in every respect, and upon the death, removal from the Territories, or insolvency of any surety, or if required by the Lieutenant-Governor, the licensee shall substitute another similar bond with the like conditions and within the time named for such purpose by notice of the said Lieutenant-Governor.

17. Upon any licensee being convicted before a justice of the peace of violating any of the terms or conditions of his license or of this Ordinance, or of insulting or ill-treating any person travelling over or desiring to travel over such ferry, or wilfully injuring or harming any property in transit across such ferry, or neglecting to repair or not removing a vessel condemned by the inspector, or not providing a suitable vessel as directed by such inspector, he shall be liable to a fine not exceeding one hundred dollars and cost of prosecution, and on non-payment thereof to be imprisoned for any period not exceeding three months, unless the fine and costs are sooner paid, and shall be further liable to forfeit his license under directions of the Lieutenant-Governor.

18. All moneys accruing from ferry license fees or bonuses, under this Ordinance, shall be paid into the General Revenue Fund of the North-West Territories.

19. No conviction shall be a bar to the ordinary civil remedies for damages in favour of the person upon whose complaint such conviction took place.

20. Every person holding a ferry license, and his sureties to the extent of the bond, shall be liable for all damages that may occur to persons and property while using such ferry from any carelessness of such licensee or his agent, or from any insufficiency in the strength or suitability of the appliances used for ferry purposes by such licensee or his agent.

21. Any person unlawfully interfering with the rights of any licensed ferryman by taking, carrying or conveying within the limit of such ferry license across the water on which the same is situate, any person or personal property, in any vessel or on any raft or other contrivance, for hire or reward, or hindering or interfering with such licenses in any way, such person shall, on conviction before a justice of the peace, be liable to the same penalties as are provided in section 17 of this Ordinance.

22. If any person using such ferry refuses to pay the proper toll or rates chargeable for ferrying himself or his property, the person holding the license of such ferry may forthwith seize any property in possession of the offender there being ferried and hold the same, and on conviction before a justice of the peace, for non-payment as aforesaid, such offender shall be liable to a fine of fifty dollars, and in default of payment to an imprisonment not exceeding two months; for the payment of which fine, and the tolls unpaid, and the costs of prosecution the property so seized shall be liable for sale under a distress warrant.

23. A return of all ferry licenses granted during the previous year, with the rates allowed, fees collected or paid, names of the parties receiving the license, together with the location and description of the ferry, shall be submitted by the Lieutenant-Governor to the North-West Council at each legislative session.

24. Every Ordinance respecting ferries heretofore in force in the North-West Territories is hereby repealed by licenses granted under the provisions of such Ordinances are hereby confirmed.

25. This Ordinance may be known as "The Ferry Ordinance of 1884."

Contributors

The assistance of the following persons is gratefully acknowledged:

Mrs. Lucy Abernathy, Barrhead; Mrs. Arline Adair, Pibroch; Mrs. & Mrs. T. Adair, Bowden; Mr. Carl J. Anderson, Brooks; J. L. Anderson, Medicine Hat; Rev. Rodney Andrews, Cardston; Ms. Lois Argue, Edmonton; Mr. Tom Baines, Calgary; Mrs. R. Barnecut, Calgary; Mr. & Mrs. J. Barraclough, Barrhead; Mr. Peter Bartoshyk, St. Paul; Mr. Fred Baxandall, Barrhead; Mr. Reg Beere, Pincher Creek; Mr. Herb Benthin, Calgary; Mrs. Natalya Bjork, Medicine Hat; Miss Isobel Bleakley, Edmonton; Mrs. Agnes Bloomquist, Scandia; Mrs. Ila Borowsky, Elk Point; Mrs. Gladys Bowman, Sundre; Mr. & Mrs. Elwood Boyd, Fawcett; Mr. Stan Boyko, Regina; Mr. W. E. Brimacombe, Vegreville; Mr. Omar Broughton, High River; Mr. Frank Burfield, Edmonton; Mrs. Louise Cameron, Calgary; Miss Isabel Campbell, Grande Prairie; Mr. C. R. Caton, Calgary; Mrs. Hazel Caverley, Calgary; Mrs. Donna Chadwick, Innisfail; Mrs. Vi Chan, Edmonton; Mrs. Florence Chappin, Prince George, B.C.; Mr. Abe Chervinski, Taber; Mr. William H. Chorney, Myrnam; Mrs. Elizabeth Clappison, Calgary; Mrs. Norine Coad, Hanna; Miss Blanche Coultis, Brooks; Mr. & Mrs. H. Coutu, Brosseau; Mr. Bruce Cropley, Warburg; Mrs. L. Crosswhite, Edmonton; Mr. Alvin Curtis, Dewberry; Mrs. Hazel Cuyler, Calgary;

Mrs. Fanny Davey, Drayton Valley; Mr. Michael Dawe, Red Deer; Mr. Charles E. Denney, Edmonton; Mr. Al Dittman, Edmonton; Mr. Ernie Domshy, Calgary; Mr. H. B. Doughty, Stettler; Mr. & Mrs. J. Dubuc, Vegreville; Mrs. Muriel Ducholke, Edmonton; Mr. H. C. Duguid, Edmonton; Mr. Jerome Durand, Carstairs; Mrs. Margherita Durling, St. Albert; Mrs. Eleanor Durnin, Dewberry; Mrs. Edgar, Calgary; Mrs. Carl Engel, Rolling Hills; Mrs. Margaret English, Two Hills; Mr. Lewis Evans, Vilna; Mrs. Annie Fedorak, Redwater; Mrs. Thelma Findlay, Lethbridge; Mrs. Jessie Finlay, Calgary; Mrs. R. C. Galloway, Two Hills; Mr. Joe Glass, Pincher Creek; Dr. Peggy Godkin, Innisfail; Mr. & Mrs. H. Gooding, Onoway; Mr. D. Gordon, Vancouver, B.C.; Mr. Glen Greenhough, Warburg; Mrs. Hazel Gregory, Pincher Creek; Mr. E. J. Hart, Banff; Mrs. Hazel Hart, Hinton; Mrs. Ella Hayes, Arrowwood; Mr. Lloyd Heaton, Trochu; Mr. Harry Hellekson, Edson; Mrs. Anna Helmer, Viking; Mrs. Hightower, Pitt Meadows, B.C.; Mr. George Hoke, Dapp; Mrs. Vera Holt, Sangudo; Mr. Dale Holtslander, Edmonton; Judge M. W. Hopkins, St. Paul; Mr. F. W. Hoskyn, Calgary; Mr. Mac Houston, Calgary; Mrs. Vi Hubbard, Edmonton; Mr. Arnold Hudson, Purple Springs; Mrs. Don Hunt, Barrhead;

Mr. Walter James, Calgary, Mr. Daniel Jantzie, Vulcan; Mrs. J. M. Jeffrey, Drumheller; Mr. Dennis Jettkant, Stony Plain; Mrs. Dorothy Johnston, Pibroch; Mr. Lewis M. Johnston, Edmonton; Mr. Peter Johnston, Drumheller; Mrs. Ida Jones, Headingley, Man.; Mr. Ray Keitges, Lethbridge; Mr. & Mrs. Tom Kempling, Drumheller; Mrs. Auley Kilcup, Gleichen; Mrs. Jean Kinch, Heinsburg; Mr. Don King, High River; Mr. R. W. Kornelson, Edmonton; Mr. Bert Laiss, Berrymoor; Mrs. R. S. Landers, Drayton Valley; Mr. James M. Layton, Cardston; Mrs. Lila Lewis, Edmonton; Mr. Alf Logan, Vermilion; Mr. Roy Logan, Calgary; Mrs. Irma Lunn, Waskatenau; Mr. T. R. McCloy, Calgary; Mr. R. A. Mackenzie, Calgary; Mrs. J. C. McLean, Irma; Mr. & Mrs. W. J. McLennan, Medicine Hat; Mrs. Ella McNeil, Fort Macleod; Mr. Howard McRae, Hinton; Mr. Paul Mabeus, Pitt, Minnesota; Ms. Jennie Machacek, Grassy Lake; Mr. E. L. Meeres, Red Deer; Mr. Mike Melnyk, St. Michael; Mr. Anatole Mercier, Bonnyville; Miss Fiona Milne, Medicine Hat; Mrs. Margaret Milne, Calgary; Mrs. J. Milner, Calgary; Mr. William Moisey, Edmonton; Mrs. Muriel Morland, Westlock; Mr. & Mrs. C. Moore, DeBolt; Mr. Ernest Moore, Calgary; Mr. R. F. Mountain, Innisfail;

J. L. Nesbitt, Brooks; Mrs. Don Nichols, Heinsburg; Mr. & Mrs. L. D. Noble, Picture Butte; Mrs. B. Parke, Creston, B.C.; Mr. F. F. Parkinson, Edmonton; Mrs. Anton Peterson, Dapp; Mr. Oscar Peterson, Marwayne; Mrs. Iva Pidcock, Kitscoty; Mr. G. E. Postill, Calgary; Mr. Ted Prescott, Willingdon; Miss Marie Randon, Fenn; Mrs. Bernice Rockwell, Morinville; Mr. & Mrs. A. Ronaghan, Islay; Mr. George L. Rotherham, Onion Lake, Sask.; Mr. Walter Rudko, Bruderheim; Mrs. M. Samis, Bon Accord; Mr. Lloyd Scheideman, Warburg; Mr. M. J. Schmitke, Whitecourt; Mrs. Eileen Schubert, Airdrie; Mr. George See, Drumheller; Mr. Tom Shandro, Edmonton; Mrs. Beth Sheehan, Grande Prairie; Mrs. Dorothy Shook, Edmonton; Mrs. Marie Sihlis, Sundre; Mrs. Laura Skarsen, Cold Lake; Mr. Edward J. Smith, Calgary; Mrs. Gladys Smith, Olds; Mr. & Mrs. R. N. Smith, Seebe; Mrs. Mabel Snider, Aldersyde; Mrs. Rosalia Snider, Aldersyde; Mr. W, D. Stephenson, Edmonton; Mrs. Eleanor Stevens, Morinville; Mr. John H. Stevenett, Innisfail; Mr. Norman D. Stewart, Edmonton; Mrs. A. Stockwell, Edmonton; Mr. E. A. Stockwell, Clandonald; Rev. Peter Stolee, Edmonton; Mr. Carl Stone, Claresholm; Mr. Leo Stutz, Cardston; Miss Betty Sutherland, Calgary;

Mrs. T. Tancowny, Waskatenau; Mrs. W.H.A. Thomas, Strathroy, Ont.; Mrs. M. C. Thomson, Edmonton; Mr. Garry Timofichuk, St. Paul; Mrs. Susie Tingle, Innisfail; Mr. A. K. Tweed, 100 Mile House, B.C.; Mrs. Edith Van Kleek, Stettler; Mrs. Ruth Walker, Hanna; Mr. Bruce Webster, Edmonton; Mrs. Beatrice Wigmore, Brooks; Mrs. Ruth Wilson, Fairview; Mrs. Jean Wood, Grande Prairie.

Index

(Note: The list of ferrymen (pp. 166-78) and names of contributors (pp. 183-84) are not indexed.)

186

187